AN
ANCHOR
FOR THE
SOUL

CHRISTIAN ART
PUBLISHERS

An Anchor for the Soul

© 2015 Christian Art Publishers
PO Box 1599, Vereeniging, 1930, RSA

First edition 2015
Second edition 2017

Devotions written by Riekert Botha

Designed by Christian Art Publishers

Set in 12 on 14 pt Minion Pro
by Christian Art Publishers

Printed in China

ISBN 978-1-4321-2496-0

19 20 21 22 23 24 25 26 27 28 – 12 11 10 9 8 7 6 5 4 3

Therefore, we who have fled to Him for refuge can have great confidence as we hold to the hope that lies before us. This hope is a strong and trustworthy anchor for our souls.

Hebrews 6:18-19

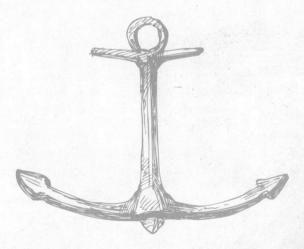

JANUARY

MIGHTIER THAN THE STORM

Mightier than the thunder of the great waters,
mightier than the breakers of the sea—
the LORD on high is mighty. Psalm 93:4

THE ALPHA AND OMEGA

God has no beginning and no end. This is a thought that is too awesome for us to grasp because our whole lives are marked out by time – by a beginning and an end. We can't imagine anything outside of this framework.

That is who God is – greater than our understanding and logic. He is greater than our thoughts. He is eternal. He is the Beginning and the End. He is greater than we can ever imagine. How comforting it is to know that our immortal God cares for mortal human beings.

"I am the Alpha and the Omega, the Beginning and the End," says the Lord, "who is and who was and who is to come, the Almighty."
Revelation 1:8 NKJV

Yours, LORD, is the greatness and the power and the glory and the majesty and the splendor, for everything in heaven and earth is Yours. Yours, LORD, is the kingdom; You are exalted as head over all.
1 Chronicles 29:11

OUR CREATOR GOD

Have you ever seen images of the Milky Way? The magnitude of the distances involved and number of stars is mind blowing – and then that's only one of many galaxies. Not only is God without a beginning or end, but He is also the Creator of the universe – a place where you and I are smaller than even the smallest unit.

Through Jesus Christ, God created the world – something that you and I can't even begin to comprehend. We can only offer Him our heartfelt praise and adoration.

In the beginning God created the heavens and the earth.
Genesis 1:1

For in Him all things were created: things in heaven and on earth, visible and invisible, whether thrones or powers or rulers or authorities; all things have been created through Him and for Him.
Colossians 1:16

GOD IS A REALITY

God is real! There are those who know that God is a reality and there are those who are unaware. Those who know that God is real are ordinary people with an extraordinary testimony. They know that God is present with them and walks with them every step they take. They know their safe harbor is in the presence of God.

We are from God, and whoever knows God listens to us; but whoever is not from God does not listen to us. This is how we recognize the Spirit of truth and the spirit of falsehood.
1 John 4:6

"You are My witnesses," declares the LORD, "and My servant whom I have chosen, so that you may know and believe Me and understand that I am He. Before Me no god was formed, nor will there be one after Me."
Isaiah 43:10

GOD IS NOT MAN-MADE

Some people think that God belongs to a denomination, but He doesn't. He is not man-made and doesn't fit into man-made structures. He is an anchor for our soul; it doesn't matter where we come from, He offers freedom and healing to all who seek refuge in Him.

God is not human, that He should lie, not a human being, that He should change His mind. Does He speak and then not act? Does He promise and not fulfill?
Numbers 23:19

I will say of the LORD, "He is my refuge and my fortress, my God, in whom I trust."
Psalm 91:2

The eternal God is your refuge, and underneath are the everlasting arms.
Deuteronomy 33:27

THE GREATEST GIFT

God gave everything He had – His Son – to set us free. This is the greatest gift that can ever be given and we marvel at the extent of God's love for us. We know that He will never leave us, especially in the midst of the storms that life tosses our way.

For God so loved the world that He gave His one and only Son, that whoever believes in Him shall not perish but have eternal life.
John 3:16

His divine power has given us everything we need for a godly life through our knowledge of Him who called us by His own glory and goodness.
2 Peter 1:3

Thanks be to God for His indescribable gift!
2 Corinthians 9:15

FOCUSED ON GOD'S PROMISE

Everything that God says and does is focused on His Promise – His Son, Jesus Christ. Every promise of redemption, restoration, healing and renewal lies in this Promise.

Christ came into this world as a stranger and was treated like a stranger, yet He brought about the salvation of God. Decide to believe in and accept God's Promise rather than to go with the world and miss this great Gift.

The wages of sin is death, but the gift of
God is eternal life in Christ Jesus our Lord.
Romans 6:23

Therefore, I urge you, brothers and sisters, in view
of God's mercy, to offer your bodies as a living
sacrifice, holy and pleasing to God – this is
your true and proper worship.
Romans 12:1

JESUS IS GOD

Jesus is God. He is the visible form of an invisible God. Jesus' words are not His unique ideas or approach. He speaks with the authority of God. Jesus is God revealed to the world.

The Son is the image of the invisible God, the firstborn over all creation.

Colossians 1:15

No one has ever seen God, but the one and only Son, who is Himself God and is in closest relationship with the Father, has made Him known.

John 1:18

Jesus answered: "Don't you know Me, Philip, even after I have been among you such a long time? Anyone who has seen Me has seen the Father."

John 14:9

BEING ACCEPTED BY GOD

The most important moment of our lives comes when we must stand before God. This is the moment when we hear that we will spend eternity in His eternal rest or that He doesn't know us. The key to this acceptance or rejection lies in His Son. Anyone who denies Jesus will be denied by God.

Ask Jesus to come into your heart to reign, then you need not fear that God won't accept you on that great day.

"Not everyone who calls out to Me, 'Lord! Lord!' will enter the Kingdom of Heaven. I will reply, 'I never knew you. Get away from Me, you who break God's laws.'"
Matthew 7:21, 23 NLT

"Whoever disowns Me before others, I will disown before My Father in heaven."
Matthew 10:33

KEEP IN FOCUS

The Father loves His Son and His focus is on Jesus. If we focus on anything except God we will see everything except God. It is important to see things from God's perspective, otherwise we see what we want to see and just ask God to bless what we want. Focus on God and everything else will fall into place.

Let us run with perseverance the race marked out for us, fixing our eyes on Jesus, the pioneer and perfecter of faith. For the joy set before Him He endured the cross, scorning its shame, and sat down at the right hand of the throne of God.
Hebrews 12:1-2

Direct me in the path of Your commands, for there I find delight. Turn my heart toward Your statutes and not toward selfish gain. Turn my eyes away from worthless things; preserve my life according to Your word.
Psalm 119:35-37

GOD'S HOUSEHOLD

To believe in the name of Jesus gives us the right to be called children of God. To embrace Jesus' position as God's Son is to become an heir yourself. What a marvelous thought that we can be called children of the Most High God.

See what great love the Father has lavished on us, that we should be called children of God! And that is what we are! The reason the world does not know us is that it did not know Him.

1 John 3:1

Consequently, you are no longer foreigners and strangers, but fellow citizens with God's people and also members of His household, built on the foundation of the apostles and prophets, with Christ Jesus Himself as the chief cornerstone.

Ephesians 2:19-20

A NEW HOME

Children of God have a new homeland, belong to a new nation and are part of a new culture that is controlled by God. God's culture is the only holy one, where people are healed, made whole, forgiven, cleansed and redeemed. A heavenly culture is the only one that gives life.

> *This is good, and pleases God our Savior, who*
> *wants all people to be saved and to come*
> *to a knowledge of the truth.*
> 1 Timothy 2:3-4

> *The Lord is not slow in keeping His promise, as*
> *some understand slowness. Instead He is patient*
> *with you, not wanting anyone to perish,*
> *but everyone to come to repentance.*
> 2 Peter 3:9

> *For Christ also suffered once for sins,*
> *the just for the unjust, that He*
> *might bring us to God.*
> 1 Peter 3:18

GOD SAVES EVERYONE

God is perfect in His holiness, but He still enters our sinful human condition in order to reach our hearts and save us. God loves everyone so much that He is willing to stoop to their level to reach them. God reaches down to a human level to save people through Jesus Christ.

To the Jews I became like a Jew, to win the Jews.
To those under the law I became like one under
the law (though I myself am not under the law),
so as to win those under the law.
1 Corinthians 9:20

We were all baptized by one Spirit so as to
form one body – whether Jews or Gentiles,
slave or free – and we were all given
the one Spirit to drink.
1 Corinthians 12:13

GOD IN US

Jesus' resurrection renewed people from the inside and for the first time opened their eyes to God's kingdom. For this reason we can understand that God is not only close to us, but within us. How privileged we are to be able to experience God in a way that was not possible before.

Do not conform to the pattern of this world, but be transformed by the renewing of your mind. Then you will be able to test and approve what God's will is – His good, pleasing and perfect will.
Romans 12:2

I pray that the eyes of your heart may be enlightened in order that you may know the hope to which He has called you, the riches of His glorious inheritance in His holy people, and His incomparably great power for us who believe.
Ephesians 1:18-19

GOD'S AUTHORITY

We learn that true power and authority are only to be found when we submit to God's authority. If we want power in the body of Christ we must submit to God and obey His commands.

Titles and accolades don't give power; obedience to God does. God gives you the opportunity to be filled with true, life-giving power if you will only bow the knee to Him in submission and obedience.

There is no authority except that which God has established. The authorities that exist have been established by God.
Romans 13:1

Does the LORD delight in burnt offerings and sacrifices as much as in obeying the LORD? To obey is better than sacrifice, and to heed is better than the fat of rams.
1 Samuel 15:22

SPEAK THE TRUTH IN LOVE

Some people say that Christians are arrogant. This isn't a very flattering thing to hear. To think that you are right and everyone else is wrong is arrogant, but to say that believers are arrogant because we believe that Jesus is the only way to heaven is not. It is believing what God says.

Ask God to help you to speak to others about Him with love and humility so that they can see the truth in what you say.

"They will treat you this way because of My name, for they do not know the One who sent Me."

John 15:21

If you are insulted because of the name of Christ, you are blessed, for the Spirit of glory and of God rests on you.

1 Peter 4:14

BURIED IN CHRIST

Through Christ our lives are hidden in God. When we die we place our spirits in the Father's hand so that we can spend eternity with Him and His Son. "So we say with confidence, 'The Lord is my helper; I will not be afraid. What can mere mortals do to me?'" (Hebrews 13:6).

Set your minds on things above, not on earthly things. You died, and your life is now hidden with Christ in God. When Christ, who is your life, appears, then you also will appear with Him in glory.
Colossians 3:2-4

Having been buried with Him in baptism, in which you were also raised with Him through your faith in the working of God, who raised Him from the dead.
Colossians 2:12

THE BODY OF CHRIST

The church is the channel through which God makes known His endless glory and holiness. The body of Christ – the church – is the glory of God on earth because Jesus is present there. If Jesus is not present no one would be able to experience God's glory or revelation of wisdom.

The only way for a body of believers to accomplish God's purpose is to bow before Jesus and to be obedient to Him in everything.

His intent was that now, through the church,
the manifold wisdom of God should be made known
to the rulers and authorities in the heavenly realms.
Ephesians 3:10

Now you are the body of Christ, and
each one of you is part of it.
1 Corinthians 12:27

GOD'S TRUE CHURCH

In Revelation, John heard that the Gentiles would take over the outer court, but that the chosen ones would be protected by God. The chosen ones are the true church of Christ that is kept safe by God Himself.

God is present where the true church is. There are so many denominations and churches, but in the end what matters is your faith in God, because the holy ones belong to Him.

"Go and measure the temple of God and the altar, with its worshipers. But exclude the outer court; do not measure it, because it has been given to the Gentiles. They will trample on the holy city for 42 months. And I will appoint my two witnesses, and they will prophesy for 1,260 days, clothed in sackcloth."
Revelation 11:1-3

God's solid foundation stands firm, sealed with this inscription: "The Lord knows those who are His."
2 Timothy 2:19

THE GLORY OF GOD

The disciples must have had some amazing experiences. The three years they spent with Jesus must have been wonderful. But they still had to wait for the power of the Holy Spirit.

They had to learn that their vision and perspectives were not enough to let God's glory descend on the nations. They must have had dreams and visions about the future, but none of them could have imagined what God had in store. It took the outpouring of the Holy Spirit and the conversion of 3,000 people in one day for them to realize what God had planned.

It isn't about us. God is and will always remain most important. It is all about Him.

Those who accepted His message were baptized,
and about three thousand were added
to their number that day.
Acts 2:41

Great is the LORD and most worthy of
praise; His greatness no one can fathom.
Psalm 145:3

FILLED TO THE BRIM

Jesus is the fulfillment of everything that God wanted to make known to man. Those who don't reject Jesus will partake of God's glory. Do you want to be filled to abundance through the only One who can give true life? Ask God to open your eyes so that you can see Him.

The Lord God is a sun and shield; the Lord bestows favor and honor; no good thing does He withhold from those whose walk is blameless.
Psalm 84:11

Therefore, since we have been justified through faith, we have peace with God through our Lord Jesus Christ, through whom we have gained access by faith into this grace in which we now stand. And we boast in the hope of the glory of God.
Romans 5:1-2

GOD IN OUR MIDST

We know that the Holy Spirit is at work when we feel God in our midst. The Holy Spirit focuses our attention on God, and those who are full of the Holy Spirit are full of God. Bow before God and ask Him to fill you with the Holy Spirit so that you can get to know our Almighty God better.

You, however, are not in the realm of the flesh but are in the realm of the Spirit, if indeed the Spirit of God lives in you. And if anyone does not have the Spirit of Christ, they do not belong to Christ.
Romans 8:9

"Where two or three gather together as My followers, I am there among them."
Matthew 18:20 NLT

Jesus replied, "The Kingdom of God can't be detected by visible signs. You won't be able to say, 'Here it is!' or 'It's over there!' For the Kingdom of God is already among you."
Luke 17:20-21

THE SOURCE OF ALL GLORY

The Holy Spirit was given to people to lead them to God. But the Holy Spirit also fulfills the important function of reminding us that God's glory doesn't revolve around us, but around Him. Our successes and failures are not important. Only God is important – and to Him we give all the glory He deserves.

"When the Advocate comes, whom I will send to you
from the Father – the Spirit of truth who goes out
from the Father – He will testify about Me."
John 15:26

"You will receive power when the Holy Spirit comes
on you; and you will be My witnesses in Jerusalem,
and in all Judea and Samaria, and to the
ends of the earth."
Acts 1:8

He, being full of the Holy Spirit, gazed into
heaven and saw the glory of God, and Jesus
standing at the right hand of God.
Acts 7:55

THE SPIRIT OF GOD

The Holy Spirit stands alongside the Father and the Son. They are of the same nature and status. The Holy Spirit is the Spirit of God, the Spirit of wisdom, the Spirit of truth, the Spirit of the Lord, the Spirit of life, our Comforter, Advocate, Helper and the Spirit of Christ.

> *There are three that testify: the Spirit, the water*
> *and the blood; and the three are in agreement.*
> *We accept human testimony, but God's testimony*
> *is greater because it is the testimony of God,*
> *which He has given about His Son.*
>
> *1 John 5:7-9*

> *The Lord is the Spirit, and where the*
> *Spirit of the Lord is, there is freedom.*
>
> *2 Corinthians 3:17*

GOD WITH US

The Holy Spirit is God with us – the indwelling Christ – the hope of glory. Through Him we come closer to God and the truth. The Holy Spirit makes our life in God practical so that we can be made holy. The Holy Spirit leads us to the safe place of refuge with God.

May God Himself, the God of peace, sanctify you through and through. May your whole spirit, soul and body be kept blameless at the coming of our Lord Jesus Christ.
1 Thessalonians 5:23

This is the one who came by water and blood – Jesus Christ. He did not come by water only, but by water and blood. And it is the Spirit who testifies, because the Spirit is the truth.
1 John 5:6

"When He, the Spirit of truth, comes, He will guide you into all the truth."
John 16:13

GOD USES THE HOLY SPIRIT

The Holy Spirit helps us to see that God wants to have a relationship with us and that Jesus has already paved the way for this to be possible. He doesn't forsake the world and is not put off by our sinful deeds. The Holy Spirit helps us to admit our need for God and encourages us to come to Him.

> *Teach me to do Your will, for You are my God;*
> *may Your good Spirit lead me on level ground.*
> *For Your name's sake, LORD, preserve my life;*
> *in Your righteousness, bring me out of trouble.*
> Psalm 143:10-11

> *Do not cast me from Your presence or take*
> *Your Holy Spirit from me. Restore to me the*
> *joy of Your salvation and grant me a*
> *willing spirit, to sustain me.*
> Psalm 51:11-12

SPIRIT OF TRUTH

When the Spirit of truth comes He will lead us in all truth. The awesomeness of the Holy Spirit's ministry is that He exalts and reveals God in the hearts of believers. He teaches us God's will and how to practically apply His teachings to our lives.

You also were included in Christ when you heard the message of truth, the gospel of your salvation. When you believed, you were marked in Him with a seal, the promised Holy Spirit, who is a deposit guaranteeing our inheritance until the redemption of those who are God's possession – to the praise of His glory.
Ephesians 1:13-14

"I will ask the Father, and He will give you another advocate to help you and be with you forever – the Spirit of truth. The world cannot accept Him, because it neither sees Him nor knows Him. But you know Him, for He lives with you and will be in you."
John 14:16-17

REVELATION OF GOD

The Holy Spirit reveals God in our everyday lives. He reveals to us everything we want to learn and know about God, because He is the Spirit of God, given to us by the Father. The Holy Spirit helps us to know Jesus and Jesus helps us to know the Father.

Jesus answered, "Very truly I tell you, no one can enter the kingdom of God unless they are born of water and the Spirit."
John 3:5

You have an anointing from the Holy One, and all of you know the truth. As for you, the anointing you received from Him remains in you, and you do not need anyone to teach you. But as His anointing teaches you about all things and as that anointing is real, not counterfeit – just as it has taught you, remain in Him.
1 John 2:20, 27

GOD IN OUR LIVES

The Holy Spirit is the ministry and presence of God in our lives. Without the Holy Spirit we are not part of God. The Holy Spirit is the practical demonstration of God in our lives.

"The Advocate, the Holy Spirit, whom the Father will send in My name, will teach you all things and will remind you of everything I have said to you."

John 14:26

Those who live according to the flesh have their minds set on what the flesh desires; but those who live in accordance with the Spirit have their minds set on what the Spirit desires. The mind governed by the flesh is death, but the mind governed by the Spirit is life and peace.

Romans 8:5-6

KNOWLEDGE OF GOD

The Holy Spirit serves an unsaved, worldly and unloving people with love and patience. He tells them who God is, what God has done and what God would like to do in their lives. The Holy Spirit convinces people that they no longer need to be slaves to sin.

Hope does not put us to shame, because God's love has been poured out into our hearts through the Holy Spirit, who has been given to us.

Romans 5:5

So I say, walk by the Spirit, and you will not gratify the desires of the flesh. For the flesh desires what is contrary to the Spirit, and the Spirit what is contrary to the flesh. They are in conflict with each other, so that you are not to do whatever you want. But if you are led by the Spirit, you are not under the law.

Galatians 5:16-18

MINISTRY OF GOD

People get very excited about the gifts of the Spirit because they are tangible and observable. But when these gifts move the focus off God, then they have lost their purpose. When people make a big deal about the gifts, they forget that they are supposed to be about God. The gifts of the Spirit are meant to be used in service to God.

There are different kinds of gifts,
but the same Spirit distributes them.
1 Corinthians 12:4

You should use whatever gift you have received to serve
others, as faithful stewards of God's grace in its various
forms. If anyone speaks, they should do so as one who
speaks the very words of God. If anyone serves, they
should do so with the strength God provides, so
that in all things God may be praised through
Jesus Christ. To Him be the glory and
the power for ever and ever. Amen.
1 Peter 4:10-11

A DEMONSTRATION OF GOD

The Holy Spirit is the connection between us and Almighty God. To see the Holy Spirit at work is the most blessed revelation on earth. The Holy Spirit demonstrates God's glory and greatness to believers.

In the same way, the Spirit helps us in our weakness. We do not know what we ought to pray for, but the Spirit Himself intercedes for us through wordless groans. He who searches our hearts knows the mind of the Spirit, because the Spirit intercedes for God's people in accordance with the will of God.

Romans 8:26-27

"I will put My Spirit in you and move you to follow My decrees and be careful to keep My laws."

Ezekiel 36:27

"God is spirit, and His worshipers must worship in the Spirit and in truth."

John 4:24

FEBRUARY

THE PILOT OF OUR SOUL

*God is our God for ever and ever; He will be
our guide even to the end.* Psalm 48:14

KNOWING GOD

Everything that we can know about God we know through Jesus. We can't know God if we don't know Jesus. Every definition of God, every revelation of God is revealed through Jesus. Jesus is the absolute definition of spiritual life and growth.

"This is the way to have eternal life – to know You, the only true God, and Jesus Christ, the one You sent to earth."
John 17:3 NLT

"All things have been committed to Me by My Father. No one knows the Son except the Father, and no one knows the Father except the Son and those to whom the Son chooses to reveal Him."
Matthew 11:27

I want to know Christ – yes, to know the power of His resurrection.
Philippians 3:10

JESUS IS THE ONLY WAY

We can only share in God's wisdom, righteousness, holiness and salvation through Jesus. To be connected to God, you must be connected to Jesus. Ask the Lord Jesus to teach you what it means to know Him.

It is because of Him that you are in Christ Jesus, who has become for us wisdom from God – that is, our righteousness, holiness and redemption. Therefore, as it is written: "Let the one who boasts boast in the Lord."

1 Corinthians 1:30-31

Be on your guard, so that you may not be carried away by the error of the lawless and fall from your secure position. But grow in the grace and knowledge of our Lord and Savior Jesus Christ. To Him be glory both now and forever! Amen.

2 Peter 3:17-18

"I AM THE DOOR"

In his gospel, John describes seven of Jesus' statements. In these statements Jesus states emphatically that He is the only way to God. In Greek the words *ego eimi* are used when someone emphasizes something as strongly as possible. Jesus uses these exact words when He says, "I am the door." What He is actually saying is, "I, and only I, am the door." No one else can do what Jesus can do; He is exclusively and without a doubt the only way to God.

> *"I am the door. If anyone enters by Me, he will be saved, and will go in and out and find pasture."*
> *John 10:9 NKJV*

> *"You are My witnesses," declares the LORD, "and My servant whom I have chosen, so that you may know and believe Me and understand that I am He. Before Me no god was formed, nor will there be one after Me."*
> *Isaiah 43:10*

"I AM THE WAY"

There is no other way of approaching God than through Jesus. There has only been one way from the beginning right up until now. Jesus alone can claim to be the only way to approach God. No one else has this right. Jesus is the only door through which we can enter God's presence. Praise the Lord, because He alone gives us access to the Father.

Jesus answered, "I am the way and the truth and the life. No one comes to the Father except through Me. If you really know Me, you will know My Father as well. From now on you do know Him and have seen Him."

John 14:6-7

Christ also suffered once for sins, the righteous for the unrighteous, to bring you to God. He was put to death in the body but made alive in the Spirit.

1 Peter 3:18

ACCESS TO GOD

The Word of God is a Person, Jesus Christ. The Power of God is a Person, Jesus Christ. The Wisdom of God is a Person, Jesus Christ. The Love of God is a Person, Jesus Christ. Everything that God gives can be found in Jesus Christ.

Jesus is the all of God and the all of God is available to us in Jesus. Through Jesus we have access to the abundance and fullness of God. Jesus is God's thirst-quenching drink for a world that is dying of thirst.

On the last and greatest day of the festival, Jesus stood and said in a loud voice, "Let anyone who is thirsty come to Me and drink. Whoever believes in Me, as Scripture has said, rivers of living water will flow from within them."

John 7:37-38

For in Christ all the fullness of the Deity lives in bodily form, and in Christ you have been brought to fullness. He is the head over every power and authority.

Colossians 2:9-10

JESUS IS THE WAY

Jesus is the only way to the Father; the only way to salvation, reconciliation and success. Spiritual maturity is not possible without Jesus. He is the true fulfillment of everything that is mature, perfect and good.

"… That all may honor the Son just as they honor the Father. Whoever does not honor the Son does not honor the Father, who sent Him."

John 5:23

I press on toward the goal to win the prize for which God has called me heavenward in Christ Jesus. All of us, then, who are mature should take such a view of things. And if on some point you think differently, that too God will make clear to you. Only let us live up to what we have already attained.

Philippians 3:14-16

THE WAY TO GOD'S FAVOR

The only way to approach the Father is through Jesus. We can only gain God's favor through Jesus. Jesus is the beloved Son in whom God is well pleased. Anything outside of Jesus falls outside God's favor. No one is able to call on God's goodwill and kindness except Jesus. Pray that God will change your thoughts, attitudes and actions to be like Jesus.

Then a cloud appeared and covered them, and
a voice came from the cloud: "This is My
Son, whom I love. Listen to Him!"
Mark 9:7

"Yes, I am the vine; you are the branches.
Those who remain in Me, and I in them, will
produce much fruit. For apart from Me you can
do nothing. Anyone who does not remain in Me
is thrown away like a useless branch and withers.
Such branches are gathered into a pile to be
burned. But if you remain in Me and My words
remain in you, you may ask for anything you
want, and it will be granted! When you produce
much fruit, you are My true disciples."
John 15:5-8 NLT

THE ROAD TO FULFILLMENT

Jesus said that He is the only way to God. No one can lay any other foundation. There are so many diverse teachings and doctrines around that it leaves one feeling light-headed, but the only teaching that leads to freedom, redemption and salvation is Jesus. There isn't another way of making right with God other than through Jesus. The Person and character of Jesus is the answer to everything. Follow where Jesus leads and walk the way of fulfillment and success.

If anyone teaches otherwise and does not agree to the sound instruction of our Lord Jesus Christ and to godly teaching, they are conceited and understand nothing. They have an unhealthy interest in controversies and quarrels about words that result in envy, strife, malicious talk, evil suspicions.
1 Timothy 6:3-4

No one can lay any foundation other than the one already laid, which is Jesus Christ.
1 Corinthians 3:11

JESUS IS THE ANSWER

Jesus is the only answer to everything that happens in and around the church – including the darkest deeds and atrocities on earth. What would Jesus do? What does Jesus say about this? Who is He? These are all questions we can ask as followers of Jesus.

The glory of God is only to be found on the "Jesus path." On what path are you traveling? Start today and walk with Jesus on the path to salvation, peace and joy.

I wait for the LORD, my whole being waits, and in His word I put my hope. I wait for the Lord more than watchmen wait for the morning.
Psalm 130:5-6

You make known to me the path of life; You will fill me with joy in Your presence, with eternal pleasures at Your right hand.
Psalm 16:11

GETTING TO KNOW JESUS

Many people say that Jesus was a great philanthropist and prophet in His time. But all evidence indicates that this is not the whole truth. He was – and is – much more than this. There was an aura around Him that made the darkest forces of evil shudder. The tragedy is that most people who go to church know the pastor, but hardly know Jesus. It's time to get to know who Jesus really is.

His divine power has given us everything we need for a godly life through our knowledge of Him who called us by His own glory and goodness. Through these He has given us His very great and precious promises, so that through them you may participate in the divine nature, having escaped the corruption in the world caused by evil desires.

2 Peter 1:3-4

I keep asking that the God of our Lord Jesus Christ, the glorious Father, may give you the Spirit of wisdom and revelation, so that you may know Him better.

Ephesians 1:17

JESUS LEADS US

Jesus is the Shepherd of our soul and He gently and lovingly leads us to safe pastures. There is no other shepherd who is as good as Jesus.

Let Jesus do what is in your best interests – be your shepherd. The world offers many false shepherds, but let Jesus lead you. He will lead you straight to the Father and to everlasting life in His presence.

"I am the good shepherd; I know My sheep and My sheep know Me – just as the Father knows Me and I know the Father – and I lay down My life for the sheep."
John 10:14-15

They will neither hunger nor thirst, nor will the desert heat or the sun beat down on them. He who has compassion on them will guide them and lead them beside springs of water.
Isaiah 49:10

A CRYSTAL CLEAR PICTURE

Jesus' mission was to reveal the Father to us. Jesus knows the heart of the Father and sees straight into our hearts. When we allow Jesus to reign in our hearts we will see things afresh and our minds will be crystal clear as He reveals the Father to us.

He has saved us and called us to a holy life – not because of anything we have done but because of His own purpose and grace. This grace was given us in Christ Jesus before the beginning of time.
2 Timothy 1:9

All this took place to fulfill what the Lord had said through the prophet: "The virgin will conceive and give birth to a son, and they will call Him Immanuel"
(which means "God with us").
Matthew 1:22-23

THE WAY TO SOMETHING GREATER

The book of John concerns the Person and character of Jesus and His calling on our lives. John doesn't speak about Jesus' miracles, but about signs. The word "sign" in Greek is equivalent to a road map: It indicates the way to something greater. Jesus' miracles were not just a show, they were meant to show us who He really is because it is here that our breakthrough lies. He is here to be God in our lives. This is the only way that we can be led to freedom and rest.

"Don't you believe that I am in the Father, and that the Father is in Me? The words I say to you I do not speak on My own authority. Rather, it is the Father, living in Me, who is doing His work. Believe Me when I say that I am in the Father and the Father is in Me; or at least believe on the evidence of the works themselves."

John 14:10-11

"Because you have so little faith. Truly I tell you, if you have faith as small as a mustard seed, you can say to this mountain, 'Move from here to there,' and it will move. Nothing will be impossible for you."

Matthew 17:20

IT'S NOT ABOUT WISHES COMING TRUE

Jesus is not there to fulfill our desires, but to be God in our lives. This is the only way that we can be led to peace and rest. Allow Jesus to be everything in your life, and remember that He isn't there to make your wishes come true, but to lead you into a life that is pleasing to Him.

Jesus performed many other signs in the presence of His disciples, which are not recorded in this book. But these are written that you may believe that Jesus is the Messiah, the Son of God, and that by believing you may have life in His name.
John 20:30-31

To those whom God has called, both Jews and Greeks, Christ the power of God and the wisdom of God.
1 Corinthians 1:24

SO MANY CHOICES

As parents it is important to allow children to make mistakes and to have the opportunity to make the right choices. With that they get to experience the consequences of their choices. God works with us in the same way. We can choose to accept Jesus into our lives; we can choose life or death and obedience or disobedience. Wrong choices don't make God love us less, but it will make our lives more difficult. Ask God to help you to choose life in Him so that you can live to the full.

Serve the LORD with fear and celebrate His rule
with trembling. For His wrath can flare up in a
moment. Blessed are all who take refuge in Him.
Psalm 2:11-12

This day I call the heavens and the earth as
witnesses against you that I have set before
you life and death, blessings and curses.
Now choose life, so that you and
your children may live.
Deuteronomy 30:19

SOMETHING THAT CAN'T BE FAKED

Just about anything in the world can be copied and falsified, except Jesus. No one can fake the life that flows from Him. There are many that say they are in Jesus, but this isn't necessarily true.

There is a big difference between those who say they are Christians and those who are true disciples. To be a true disciple and to receive the life that flows from Him, you must walk as He did. Are you walking in Jesus' footsteps as a true disciple?

Whoever claims to live in Him must live as Jesus did.
1 John 2:6

We are God's handiwork, created in Christ Jesus
to do good works, which God prepared
in advance for us to do.
Ephesians 2:10

JESUS IS THE TRUTH

Pilate asked Jesus, "What is truth?" (John 18:38). Jesus said, "The reason I was born and came into the world is to testify to the truth" (verse 37). To go to church and to know portions of the Bible, to be acquainted with important people in religious circles, to belong to a big congregation and to know how to string Scripture verses together to suit the situation never saved anyone. The Person and character of Jesus Christ define truth. People who are in Jesus are in the truth. Jesus' teaching on every facet of life is the definition of what is true and false. Turn to Jesus and ask Him to reveal His truth to you.

Guide me in Your truth and teach me,
for You are God my Savior, and my
hope is in You all day long.
Psalm 25:5

The law was given through Moses; grace
and truth came through Jesus Christ.
John 1:17

YOUR RIGHTS DON'T SET YOU FREE

To stand on your rights and to stand on the truth are two different things. Rights never made anyone truly free – only the Truth can set us free. Only Jesus can set our hearts and souls free from the shackles of sin that bind us down.

The Word became flesh and made His dwelling among us. We have seen His glory, the glory of the one and only Son, who came from the Father, full of grace and truth.
John 1:14

Whoever lives by the truth comes into the light, so that it may be seen plainly that what they have done has been done in the sight of God.
John 3:21

IN THE TRUTH OF GOD

Those who are in Jesus are in the truth. Jesus' teachings on every facet of our lives give us the definition of what is true and false. Turn to Jesus and ask Him to reveal His truth to you so that you can live in the truth.

Send me Your light and Your faithful care,
let them lead me; let them bring me to Your
holy mountain, to the place where You dwell.
Psalm 43:3

Continue your love to those who know you,
your righteousness to the upright in heart.
Psalm 36:10

You were taught with regard to your former way
of life, to put off your old self, which is being
corrupted by its deceitful desires; to be made
new in the attitudes of your minds; and to
put on the new self, created to be like God
in true righteousness and holiness.
Ephesians 4:22-24

IS OUR TRUTH TRUE?

As humans we sit with a great mix of truths, half-truths and lies which build our thoughts on who we think we are and how we see the world around us. The greatest part on which we build our lives, however, is not true.

We attach our value to achievements, appearance, associations, money, popularity, possessions and qualifications. These things are all lies because God does not determine our value based on these things. Ask God to enlighten your life with His truth and be prepared to remove all lies and untruths from your thinking.

We will be ready to punish every act of
disobedience, once your obedience is complete.
2 Corinthians 10:6

Teach me Your way, LORD, that I may rely
on Your faithfulness; give me an undivided
heart, that I may fear Your name.
Psalm 86:11

THE BATTLE BETWEEN TRUTH AND SELF-PRESERVATION

The greatest drive in our lives is self-preservation. We strive for it and we fight for it. We can sometimes be so wrong and yet still continue fighting for it (or the false image of preservation that we have). This is where self-preservation and truth begin to clash. Jesus says that if we want to follow Him, we must deny ourselves. When you stand in God's truth, you can't be self-seeking, because God's truth is the opposite of jealousy and selfishness. God's truth is peace-loving, courteous, compassionate, fruit-bearing, impartial and sincere.

For those who are self-seeking and who reject the truth and follow evil, there will be wrath and anger.
Romans 2:8

Then Jesus said to His disciples, "Whoever wants to be My disciple must deny themselves and take up their cross and follow Me."
Matthew 16:24

EMBRACE THE TRUTH

When we aren't in control, can we be sure that God is? Think about it – we link Jesus' abilities to our own, something we do unconsciously.

When all is going well with us and we are prosperous, we think Jesus is good and wonderful. When disaster strikes and we are in the midst of a crisis, Jesus is no longer so good and wonderful. It is enlightening to recognize this in our own lives because it helps us to embrace the truth.

Ask God to help you see this in your own life so that you can change and embrace God's absolute goodness and control.

Sanctify them by the truth; Your word is truth.
John 17:17

If we claim to have fellowship with Him and yet walk in the darkness, we lie and do not live out the truth.
1 John 1:6

TRUST JESUS COMPLETELY

God's truth is not dependent on our emotional state. Even in the midst of a situation we have lost total control over, Jesus is still the King of kings and He oversees our affairs. We can completely submit to His leading.

Give yourself to Jesus and trust Him, knowing that He has complete wisdom and control and will work things out as is best for you.

We know that in all things God works
for the good of those who love Him, who
have been called according to His purpose.
Romans 8:28

Stand firm then, with the belt of truth
buckled around your waist, with the
breastplate of righteousness in place.
Ephesians 6:14

ONLY THE TRUTH WILL SET YOU FREE

Truth is the answer to everything. Our lives are so interspersed with lies and corruption that the search for truth has become a highly specialized task. This is so because truth has become so obscured and blurred that it takes an expert to find it. We spend a lot of time twisting and reshaping the truth so that we can do what we want without bearing the consequences. Then comes the realization that we can't fight the truth anymore because we are sinking deeper and deeper into bondage.

Ask the Lord to open your eyes so that you can start to stand on His truth and live a life of true freedom from the bonds of sin.

If we claim to be without sin, we
deceive ourselves and the truth is not in us.
1 John 1:8

"Then you will know the truth,
and the truth will set you free."
John 8:32

FREEDOM AND PEACE

When a crisis hits our lives we flee from our nest of lies and reach out desperately and grab the truth, "Lord, help!" The result? Freedom! When we embrace the truth and turn to God, He sets us free from all the lies and worries that kept us captive for so long. The result of this is a peace that gently rains down on us and fills our hearts with rest and calm.

There are six things the LORD hates, seven that are detestable to Him: haughty eyes, a lying tongue, hands that shed innocent blood, a heart that devises wicked schemes, feet that are quick to rush into evil, a false witness who pours out lies and a person who stirs up conflict in the community.

Proverbs 6:16-19

For what the law was powerless to do because it was weakened by the flesh, God did by sending His own Son in the likeness of sinful flesh to be a sin offering. And so He condemned sin in the flesh.

Romans 8:3

HEALED BY THE TRUTH

Are you in search of the truth? Turn to Jesus and be set free from the terrible things in your heart and life. You will be healed from the pollution in your soul.

Call on the Lord and you will see the invisible become visible. Then go and seek His disciples. Tell them about what happened to you. Allow the Lord to set you free and heal you.

> *Seek the LORD while He may be found;*
> *call on Him while He is near.*
> Isaiah 55:6

> *We declare God's wisdom, a mystery that has*
> *been hidden and that God destined for*
> *our glory before time began.*
> 1 Corinthians 2:7

MY TRUTH IS THE MOST IMPORTANT

We want the authority to determine the truth for ourselves and yet we fail again and again. Can you see how senseless this is?

We sweep God's truth off the table and replace it with our own theories of what is true and false. What does it matter that our arguments sound so intellectual and progressive, and yet they can't guarantee any lasting results except alienation and loss?

Our truth is not the most important. There is only freedom and healing in God's truth in Christ Jesus. To be right doesn't mean anything, but to be in the truth means everything.

Didn't it belong to you before it was sold?
And after it was sold, wasn't the money at
your disposal? What made you think of doing
such a thing? You have not lied just to
human beings but to God.
Acts 5:4

Your righteousness is an everlasting
righteousness, and Your law is truth.
Psalm 119:142

TRUTH OR STUMBLING BLOCK?

The consequences of people's actions betray the source. There are many undercurrents among believers about what to believe and do. How are we to know? Look at the consequences: if it causes arguments, jealousy and harsh words, then something is seriously wrong. If our ideas and "truths" are far from God, only the above-mentioned traits will be present in our hearts.

Whatever the argument or situation, the end result will reveal whether Jesus was present or not. Is your truth really true or a stumbling block? Does it speak the Spirit of Christ or not?

Keep reminding God's people of these things.
Warn them before God against quarreling about
words; it is of no value, and only ruins those who listen.
2 Timothy 2:14

Do your best to present yourself to God as one
approved, a worker who does not need to be
ashamed and who correctly handles the word of truth.
2 Timothy 2:15

A LOVE FOR THE TRUTH

A person's love for the truth is tested to the utmost when it means you must deny yourself to stand in the truth. It's so radical that you won't be able to say, "I love the truth, but I love myself more." Jesus says that if you say this, you don't really love the truth. To love the truth and to deny ourselves is to be free in God.

> "When He, the Spirit of truth, comes, He will guide you into all the truth. He will not speak on His own; He will speak only what He hears, and He will tell you what is yet to come."
>
> John 16:13

> Instead, speaking the truth in love, we will grow to become in every respect the mature body of Him who is the head, that is, Christ.
>
> Ephesians 4:15

MARCH

HE STILLS THE STORM

*They cried out to the Lᴏʀᴅ in their trouble, and
He brought them out of their distress.
He stilled the storm to a whisper; the waves of the
sea were hushed. They were glad when it grew
calm, and He guided them to their
desired haven.* Psalm 107:6, 29-30

JESUS, THE PRINCE OF PEACE

Peace is a deep-seated need in every person's life. People desire peace with their family, children, spouse, themselves and with God. We all long for security and quietness. Jesus gives this kind of peace and those who believe in Him can possess this kind of peace. It is a divine peace that exists with those who have Jesus in their lives and midst.

"Peace I leave with you; My peace I give you.
I do not give to you as the world gives. Do not
let your hearts be troubled and do not be afraid."
John 14:27

To us a child is born, to us a son is given,
and the government will be on His shoulders.
And He will be called Wonderful Counselor,
Mighty God, Everlasting Father, Prince of Peace.
Isaiah 9:6

JESUS IS PEACE

Jesus not only gives peace, but He is peace. Peace is not something that He hands out like a food hamper, it is something within Him. When people feel safe they are filled with peace. Jesus' power in the life of a believer is His source of peace. The world can't receive this kind of peace because it does not submit to Him. When the Almighty Ruler is in your midst, the authority, peace and calmness of the Prince of Peace is with you. The peace of Jesus reigns.

The mind governed by the flesh is death, but
the mind governed by the Spirit is life and peace.
The mind governed by the flesh is hostile to God;
it does not submit to God's law, nor can it do so.
Romans 8:6-7

Grace and peace to you from God
our Father and the Lord Jesus Christ.
1 Corinthians 1:3

THE THIEF OF PEACE

There are usually unpleasant consequences when a believer's family are not followers of Jesus. This causes a conflict of interest – like that between darkness and light. Darkness wants to hide and remain independent of God, while light wants to be open and intimate with God. This conflict brings strife and disunity. Peace can only descend when the light dims or when the darkness becomes light. When you bow before Jesus as Lord and Savior, His light shines into your life.

People loved darkness instead of light because their deeds were evil. Everyone who does evil hates the light, and will not come into the light for fear that their deeds will be exposed. But whoever lives by the truth comes into the light, so that it may be seen plainly that what they have done has been done in the sight of God.

John 3:19-21

Open the gates that the righteous nation may enter, the nation that keeps faith. You will keep in perfect peace those whose minds are steadfast, because they trust in You.

Isaiah 26:2-3

PEACE UNDER CONTROL

If you have lost peace you need to regain it, because you can't carry on without the peace of God in your heart. Our life begins to shake when we don't have the protection of God around our heart. It is our responsibility to see that the peace of God reigns in our heart. We can only do this by placing ourselves completely under God's authority and control.

*Let the peace of Christ rule in your hearts, since
as members of one body you were called to peace.
And be thankful.*
Colossians 3:15

*May the Lord of peace Himself give you peace at all
times and in every way. The Lord be with all of you.*
2 Thessalonians 3:16

The God of peace be with you all.
Romans 15:13

THE PEACE OF GOD

Popular thinking considers peace as the absence of problems and crises. Jesus sees peace as the presence of God. Where God reigns, there is peace. This means that believers can experience peace even in the mist of life-threatening situations.

Jesus is completely in control and He never stops working in the lives of believers, even though it might be dark and negative. The peace that we receive from God is not dependent on circumstances or the outcome of a crisis, but is dependent on His presence.

Even though I walk through the darkest valley,
I will fear no evil, for You are with me;
Your rod and Your staff, they comfort me.
Psalm 23:4

"I have told you these things, so that in Me
you may have peace. In this world you
will have trouble. But take heart!
I have overcome the world."
John 16:33

ANYTHING FOR PEACE

Most people hate conflict. People might sometimes do things they dislike just to keep the peace. They might be stressed out, but they don't want to do anything to rock the boat, because they fear conflict. People like this might even deny or ignore Jesus if it means keeping the peace with others.

It is good to be peace-loving, but not at Jesus' expense. We need to be forgiven for this sin and freed from the fear that results from it. Freedom begins when you submit to Jesus' authority, despite the consequences it may bring.

Fear of man will prove to be a snare, but
whoever trusts in the LORD is kept safe.
Proverbs 29:25

Those who flatter their neighbors are
spreading nets for their feet.
Proverbs 29:5

THE GREATEST STUMBLING BLOCK TO PEACE

The biggest stumbling block to having joy and peace in your life is you. It really takes a divine revelation to see this, because we always think we are right and everyone else is wrong. The best way to fight pride and selfishness is to give yourself to Jesus. If you want to do what Jesus tells you, you need to stop being self-righteous.

Do nothing out of selfish ambition or vain conceit. Rather, in humility value others above yourselves, not looking to your own interests but each of you to the interests of others.
Philippians 2:3-4

Surely Your goodness and love will follow me all the days of my life, and I will dwell in the house of the LORD forever.
Psalm 23:6

REST IN JESUS

Jesus is the true Sabbath of God. Jesus is God's rest for every soul, long after time and days have passed. We can't find rest for our souls unless we find it in Jesus. Soul rest comes from giving yourself fully to Jesus. If we don't do this we aren't in God's rest and we can't please Him. To give everything to Jesus instead of doing it yourself is to find peace in Him.

Submit to God and be at peace with Him; in this way prosperity will come to you. Accept instruction from His mouth and lay up His words in your heart.
Job 22:21-22

There remains, then, a Sabbath-rest for the people of God; for anyone who enters God's rest also rests from their works, just as God did from His.
Hebrews 4:9-10

MY SOUL FINDS REST IN GOD ALONE

We get so side-tracked by all kinds of man-made rules and regulations that we don't focus on what is important – the peace of God that is in Christ Jesus. Trying to please God without resting in Jesus is always bound to fail. There is a wonderful soul rest for those who seek rest in Jesus – free from the yoke of man-made religion and systems.

"Come to Me, all you who are weary and burdened, and I will give you rest. Take My yoke upon you and learn from Me, for I am gentle and humble in heart, and you will find rest for your souls. For My yoke is easy and My burden is light."

Matthew 11:28-30

Truly my soul finds rest in God;
my salvation comes from Him.

Psalm 62:1

ENTER INTO PEACE

People go to great lengths to please and satisfy God, but their efforts are inadequate and fruitless. God has already done everything – He has opened the new and living way so that we can find rest for our souls. Everyone who enters this way lives in it.

There is nothing that we can do to impress God. Jesus has already done what needed to be done. To accept Jesus into your heart is to enter God's true rest, without which there can be no peace, no salvation and no forgiveness. Jesus is the peace and rest of God. Find Jesus and you will find rest, for now and for ever.

"In repentance and rest is your salvation,
in quietness and trust is your strength,
but you would have none of it."
Isaiah 30:15

In vain you rise early and stay up late,
toiling for food to eat – for He grants
sleep to those He loves.
Psalm 127:2

"PEACE BE WITH YOU!"

Jesus' greeting to the people He met was "Peace be with you!" Even when Jesus appeared as the image of the invisible God to Gideon in the Old Testament and later to John, He greeted them with "Peace be with you." There has always been peace in the Person and character of Jesus. Remember that Jesus can also minister to you with His peace.

Again Jesus said, "Peace be with you! As the Father has sent Me, I am sending you."
John 20:21

Grace and peace to you from God our Father and the Lord Jesus Christ.
Galatians 1:3

The Lord gives strength to His people; the Lord blesses His people with peace.
Psalm 29:11

LOVE ALLOWS A CHOICE

Through Jesus Christ we were created by God and we are loved by Him. God loves us tremendously, but He lets us decide whether we will love Him back. The consequences of this decision are demonstrated very clearly. The one choice results in life and peace in God's presence. The other results in death and devastation. God loves us enough not to force us to choose Him, even though we often stubbornly choose death. He still goes to great lengths to give us another chance. Choose life and peace today.

This day I call the heavens and the earth as witnesses
against you that I have set before you life and death,
blessings and curses. Now choose life, so that you
and your children may live.
Deuteronomy 30:19

Give thanks to the God of gods.
His love endures forever.
Psalm 136:2

LOVE BECAME PERFECT

The punishment of sin is death. The only way that we can escape God's punishment is if someone else stands in for us and dies in our place. This person must be free from sin – otherwise they die for their own sins, not the sins of the one they are trying to help. From the beginning God knew that Jesus would be this perfect Person. Jesus became the perfect sacrifice that was offered on our behalf to save us from death. This is perfect love.

The next day John saw Jesus coming toward him and said, "Look, the Lamb of God, who takes away the sin of the world!"
John 1:29

Walk in the way of love, just as Christ loved us and gave Himself up for us as a fragrant offering and sacrifice to God.
Ephesians 5:2

A DEMONSTRATION OF LOVE

The greatest demonstration of love was when Jesus died on the cross for our sins. Never, since then, has there been a greater act of love. The greatest testimony of victory over Satan and sin is seen in the lives of those who have been set free through Jesus. We are to live lives showing the same love and humility that Jesus had and in so doing sow seeds of peace wherever we go.

God demonstrates His own love for us in this:
While we were still sinners, Christ died for us.
Romans 5:8

This is love: not that we loved God,
but that He loved us and sent His Son
as an atoning sacrifice for our sins.
1 John 4:10

THE KING OF OUR HEARTS

Jesus could blurt out all of our faults and wrongdoings, but He doesn't, because this isn't His goal. His goal is love and truth from which all life and purity flows. Put on the love and character of Jesus when you interact with others and you will find peace within yourself and between yourself and others.

*Sow righteousness for yourselves, reap the fruit
of unfailing love, and break up your unplowed
ground; for it is time to seek the LORD, until He
comes and showers His righteousness on you.*
Hosea 10:12

*No one has ever seen God;
but if we love one another, God lives
in us and His love is made complete in us.*
1 John 4:12

MATTERS OF THE HEART

"I wish I was overweight!" Not words you often hear. Usually people spend a lot of money, drink pills and run many miles to lose weight. But with matters of the heart, things work differently.

Jesus weighs our hearts. This means that He tests the integrity of our inner selves. A lightweight heart is one that stubbornly shuts God out and refuses to allow Him to reign. A heavyweight heart is one that thirsts for God, like a deer pants for water. Take a look at your own heart. What does it weigh?

Love the LORD your God with all your heart
and with all your soul and with all your strength.
Deuteronomy 6:5

As the deer longs for streams
of water, so I long for You, O God.
Psalm 42:1 NLT

WIN THE HEAVYWEIGHT TROPHY!

A heavyweight heart is one that testifies that Jesus is the true King and that He is worthy to reign over every part of our lives. Qualifications, money, status, possessions and honor don't make you a heavyweight. It's your heart and whether you are really seeking Jesus that determines your weight. May you have a heavyweight heart because that's the only way to true life!

Do everything in love.
1 Corinthians 16:14

Whoever pursues righteousness
and love finds life, prosperity and honor.
Proverbs 21:21

May the Lord make your love increase and
overflow for each other and for everyone else.
1 Thessalonians 3:12

A SINCERE LOVE FOR OTHERS

No school or educational institution can teach you how to love. We are programmed to judge the "purity" of someone's teachings without considering the command to love others from a pure heart, not judge them. We should have a sincere desire to love others and in so doing inspire others to live a life of love. Our hearts should strive to love instead of judging.

*"Do not judge, or you too will be judged. For
in the same way you judge others, you will be judged,
and with the measure you use, it will be measured to you."*
Matthew 7:1-2

*Now that you have purified yourselves
by obeying the truth so that you have sincere love
for each other, love one another deeply, from the heart.*
1 Peter 1:22

LOVE ON FIRE

The Holy Spirit works in us to promote love. The fruit of God's cleansing is a love that is on fire in a pure heart. This is God in us because God is love. True divine cleansing always leads to a deeper relationship with God. Greater love leads to greater purity and holiness.

Flee the evil desires of youth and pursue righteousness, faith, love and peace, along with those who call on the Lord out of a pure heart.
2 Timothy 2:22

We know and rely on the love God has for us. God is love. Whoever lives in love lives in God, and God in them.
1 John 4:16

"A new commandment I give you: Love one another. As I have loved you, so you must love one another."
John 13:34

HOW MUCH DOES GOD LOVE ME?

People say that Jesus' love is not measurable, but it is. In Ephesians, Paul prays that the church in Ephesus might know the width, length, height and depth of God's love. One way to understand this is to say that God loves us so much that nothing can stop Him from loving us. Jesus hates sin, but He loves us more. Never think that your sin is too bad to keep Him from loving you. Nothing can separate us from God's love …

May you have the power to understand,
as all God's people should, how wide, how long,
how high, and how deep his love is. May you
experience the love of Christ, though it is too
great to understand fully. Then you will be
made complete with all the fullness of life
and power that comes from God.
Ephesians 3:18-19 NLT

Above all, love each other deeply, because
love covers over a multitude of sins.
1 Peter 4:8

A LOVE THAT NEVER RUNS DRY

No sin is so great that it can stand between you and God's love. Isn't this amazing! What would make you stop loving your child? If your child was a murderer, a thief, a drug addict or rejected God, would you still love them? These things would tear your heart in two and cause you immense suffering and heartbreak, but you would still love your child. Accordingly, you can begin to understand the love that Jesus has for each one of us.

I am convinced that neither death nor life, neither angels nor demons, neither the present nor the future, nor any powers, neither height nor depth, nor anything else in all creation, will be able to separate us from the love of God that is in Christ Jesus our Lord.

Romans 8:38-39

Give thanks to the LORD for His unfailing love and His wonderful deeds for mankind.

Psalm 107:31

LOVE IS NOT A TICKET TO SIN

Jesus loves us no matter what we do. But this fact doesn't mean that we can do what we want because we know that Jesus still loves us. There are other factors that we need to remember. The first fact is that God will judge all sin – without exception. Jesus' love is huge in all respects, but He does judge our sin because there is a penalty for every injustice that we commit towards others. God punishes all unrighteousness because it is rebellion against Him. There is no excuse for sin.

"I have loved you with an everlasting love; I have drawn you with unfailing kindness."
Jeremiah 31:3

"I will search for the lost and bring back the strays. I will bind up the injured and strengthen the weak. I will shepherd the flock with justice."
Ezekiel 34:16

GOD LOVES YOU IN SPITE OF YOU

God's love for us is endless, but our actions do have consequences. So even though God loves us, we reap what we sow and we need to face the consequences of our actions. Love is not like a huge smoke screen that hides our rebellion and disobedience from God. Love says, "Even though you disobey Me and heap up consequences for your deeds, I still love you."

Love is patient, love is kind. It does not envy, it does not boast, it is not proud. It does not dishonor others, it is not self-seeking, it is not easily angered, it keeps no record of wrongs. Love does not delight in evil but rejoices with the truth. It always protects, always trusts, always hopes, always perseveres.

1 Corinthians 13:4-7

The LORD is good and His love endures forever; His faithfulness continues through all generations.

Psalm 100:5

LOVE IS THE ANSWER

"What must I do for God to love me?" is a question many ask. The answer is, "Nothing." Even when we were sinners – enemies of God – He showed us His love by sending Jesus to die for us. The world is sin-infested and really ugly, yet God loves the world. This is amazing! This is pure undeserved, unconditional love and it is the answer to all the trauma, drama and agony of sin.

For God so loved the world that He gave
His one and only Son, that whoever believes in
Him shall not perish but have eternal life.
John 3:16

You were once far away from God. You were His
enemies, separated from Him by your evil thoughts and
actions. Yet now He has reconciled you to Himself through
the death of Christ in His physical body. As a result,
He has brought you into His own presence, and
you are holy and blameless as you stand before
Him without a single fault.
Colossians 1:21-22 NLT

LOVE IN OUR HEARTS

Every person who is won through God's unconditional love receives love. Can we love as God loves? Yes. The same love that was poured into our hearts when we were born again enables us to love others with the same love that God offers us. This is a gift from God.

> *"My command is this: Love each other*
> *as I have loved you. Greater love has no one*
> *than this: to lay down one's life for one's friends."*
> John 15:12-13

> *Sing to the LORD, all the earth; proclaim His*
> *salvation day after day. Declare His glory among*
> *the nations, His marvelous deeds among all peoples.*
> *For great is the LORD and most worthy of praise;*
> *He is to be feared above all gods.*
> 1 Chronicles 16:23-25

THE DEFINING CHARACTERISTIC OF BELIEVERS

God gives us the love we need to love others. When we are born again God pours His love into our hearts through the Holy Spirit and then says, "Love your enemies," in other words, "Love unconditionally as I do." This is what distinguishes us from the world. The world can't love unconditionally. The world can't fabricate love, because it is the defining characteristic of Christians. This is indisputable evidence of God's work in a person's life.

"Your love for one another will prove to the world that you are My disciples."
John 13:35 NLT

Your unfailing love will last forever.
Your faithfulness is as enduring as the heavens.
Psalm 89:2 NLT

UNCONDITIONAL LOVE

To think that God calls us to love unconditionally is an awesome thought, but to see this put into practice brings the depths of God to the forefront. It doesn't matter what other people do, we must always love them as God has loved us. To withhold love is never justified in any circumstances.

Now these three remain: faith, hope and love.
But the greatest of these is love.
1 Corinthians 13:13

Let love and faithfulness never leave you;
bind them around your neck, write them on
the tablet of your heart.
Proverbs 3:3

Love must be sincere. Hate what is evil;
cling to what is good.
Romans 12:9

WHAT DOES IT MEAN TO LOVE?

Love never acts in a loveless manner. Love never says things from hurt and bitter feelings in order to hurt others. Love never returns violence for violence. Love never turns to hate when it bleeds. Love does what is wise and loving. Love remains obedient to God, whatever happens.

Dear friends, let us love one another, for love comes from God. Everyone who loves has been born of God and knows God.
1 John 4:7

We love because He first loved us. Whoever claims to love God yet hates a brother or sister is a liar. For whoever does not love their brother and sister, whom they have seen, cannot love God, whom they have not seen.
1 John 4:19-20

PUNISHMENT OR GRACE?

Is it unloving to repay people for their transgressions or is it just and fair? When people turn against the Almighty God and reject Him and He punishes them accordingly, is it unloving and irrational? God does punish, but He loves us so much that He doesn't want to punish, but rather save us. God will punish sin, but He gives us a choice – punishment or grace. Choose today to accept God's gracious hand and let Him lead you to peace and life in abundance.

The grace of God has appeared that offers salvation to all people.
Titus 2:11

I remember my affliction and my wandering, the bitterness and the gall. I well remember them, and my soul is downcast within me. Yet this I call to mind and therefore I have hope: Because of the LORD's great love we are not consumed, for His compassions never fail.
Lamentations 3:19-22

LOVE IS NOT BASED ON FEELINGS

It is important to distinguish between true love and infatuation, even within the church situation. In some Christian circles there is a tendency to go for emotional and "goose-flesh" experiences that do not focus lovingly on Jesus Christ. It is not wrong to experience and feel, but Jesus is much more than this.

Your relationship with God does not depend on the right atmosphere. It is a result of the Holy Spirit in your life. True love does not depend on emotions or experiences.

Hope does not put us to shame, because God's love has been poured out into our hearts through the Holy Spirit, who has been given to us.
Romans 5:5

The LORD your God is with you, the Mighty Warrior who saves. He will take great delight in you; in His love He will no longer rebuke you, but will rejoice over you with singing.
Zephaniah 3:17

INFATUATION OR TRUE LOVE?

The person who is infatuated with love will try everything to hold on to the feelings and experience of being in love. Such a person will leave their mate as soon as the feelings of love vanish. True love is being prepared to go through crises and hard times to make the relationship work. Is your relationship with God based on true love or are you in love with being in love?

Love does not rejoice about injustice but rejoices whenever the truth wins out. Love never gives up, never loses faith, is always hopeful, and endures through every circumstance.
1 Corinthians 13:6-7 NLT

Satisfy us in the morning with your unfailing love, that we may sing for joy and be glad all our days.
Psalm 90:14

Whoever does not love does not know God, because God is love. This is how God showed His love: He sent His one and only Son into the world that we might live through Him.
1 John 4:8-9

APRIL

AN ANCHOR OF HOPE

*Therefore, we who have fled to Him for refuge
can have great confidence as we hold to the hope
that lies before us. This hope is a strong and
trustworthy anchor for our souls.* Hebrews 6:18-19

GOD GIVES HOPE

God changes our lives daily. He regularly changes bad circumstances into something good. The only condition is that you must be walking with Him. You can't expect God to turn a crisis situation around if you aren't following Him. God is mighty enough to change any dire situation you find yourself in into one in which you come out an as overcomer. No one can achieve this through sheer determination alone. Only God can accomplish this.

"I have told you these things, so that in Me you may have peace. In this world you will have trouble. But take heart! I have overcome the world."

John 16:33

You, God, see the trouble of the afflicted; You consider their grief and take it in hand. The victims commit themselves to You; You are the helper of the fatherless.

Psalm 10:14

TRUSTING GOD IN THE MIDST OF DEVASTATION

The devil sows death and lies wherever he goes in this world. But this doesn't mean that God isn't in control. These things happen because God has given man the power and authority to rule ourselves, while the devil has the authority to rule over the earth. God has set boundaries within which this devastation may take place, and He has sent Jesus to save us from this destruction. We may not always understand all this, but we place our trust in God and know that He is in control and that He has a greater plan for us.

Therefore, just as sin entered the world through one man, and death through sin, and in this way death came to all people, because all sinned.
Romans 5:12

The creation was subjected to frustration, not by its own choice, but by the will of the one who subjected it, in hope that the creation itself will be liberated from its bondage to decay and brought into the freedom and glory of the children of God.
Romans 8:20-21

THE GREAT DOCTOR

We are surrounded by tragedy every day. People are born with disabilities, have accidents and become ill. This is the world in which we live. It overwhelms our existence and way of thinking. When try to make sense of the despair around us, we can end up feeling hopeless and even aggressive. We become angry with God because we don't understand what is happening around us.

Man and all his innovation and technology stands helpless in the face of tragedy. But the Lord is never limited or confined by trauma and tragedy. Jesus is more than a Band-Aid for the world, He is the great Doctor.

I say to myself, "The LORD is my portion;
therefore I will wait for Him."
Lamentations 3:24

The LORD is good, a refuge in times of trouble.
He cares for those who trust in Him.
Nahum 1:7

GOD IS THE ANSWER

Is everything that happens to us good? No, definitely not! Terrible things happen to people in this world. Even worse, people do horrible things to each other. Everything is not good. The Bible in no way suggests that believers will live problem-free, easy-going lives.

Not everything that happens to us is good, but everything can work out for the best. God can turn a devastating situation around. What would otherwise be unbearable suffering, God can make into a victory in your life. God is the answer even though we don't have all the answers.

We know that God causes everything to work together
for the good of those who love God and are called
according to His purpose for them.
Romans 8:28 NLT

I heard a loud voice from the throne saying,
"Look! God's dwelling place is now among the
people, and He will dwell with them. They will be
His people, and God Himself will be with
them and be their God."
Revelation 21:3

JESUS IS UNLIMITED

Some of the things that we buckle under are disabilities, shortages and losses. There is too little money, too little food, too little love, too little patience, too little courtesy and too little respect. But Jesus is way above any shortages. He is not limited by these things. He can meet our need in any situation, we need only trust Him.

Blessed is the one who trusts in the LORD,
who does not look to the proud, to those who
turn aside to false gods.
Psalm 40:4

As Scripture says, "Anyone who believes
in Him will never be put to shame."
Romans 10:11

In the day of my trouble I will call upon
You, for You will answer me.
Psalm 86:7 NKJV

TRUST GOD, NOT SCIENCE

God is the most unscientific scientist. He has set in place all the laws in nature, but is Himself not bound to them at all. How scientific is it to raise someone from the dead, turn water into wine and make iron float on water? It isn't scientific, but that doesn't stop God.

We are often confronted with problems that get dictated to by the world. Earthquakes, floods, storms, tsunamis, droughts – whatever you can think of. Jesus is high above all these things. Our faith in Him is faith in God who is unlimited. God is greater than the limitations in our lives today and He wants to reveal this to you. Trust Him, more than you trust in science.

When you pass through the waters,
I will be with you; and when you pass through
the rivers, they will not sweep over you. When you walk
through the fire, you will not be burned.
Isaiah 43:2

Though I walk in the midst of trouble,
You preserve my life. You stretch out Your
hand against the anger of my foes; with
Your right hand You save me.
Psalm 138:7

JESUS IS MY EXPECTATION

To allow God to do His will in your life is the highest form of worship. Therefore we must trust that God is our healer, even if we are not cured. We must trust that He loves us, even when circumstances are screaming the opposite. We must trust that He will pick us up, even when we are still lying bruised on the ground. We must stop placing expectations on God and simply start to trust Him. He alone is worthy to have complete control over our lives.

No one who hopes in You will ever be put to shame,
but shame will come on those who are
treacherous without cause.
Psalm 25:3

The LORD will vindicate me; Your love, LORD,
endures forever – do not abandon the
works of Your hands.
Psalm 138:8

WHO CONTROLS YOUR LIFE?

The greatest turning point in your life will happen when you allow Jesus to be God in your life, even though He doesn't do exactly what you want Him to do. Even though it doesn't always seem like it, Jesus is always in control. Trust Jesus with your life, no matter how tough things may be.

> *"God blesses those who do not*
> *turn away because of Me."*
> *Matthew 11:6 NLT*

> *I remain confident of this: I will see the goodness of*
> *the Lord in the land of the living. Wait for the LORD;*
> *be strong and take heart and wait for the LORD.*
> *Psalm 27:13-14*

> *Those who know Your name trust in You, for You,*
> *LORD, have never forsaken those who seek You.*
> *Psalm 9:10*

TRUSTING IN GOD

In order to trust God, we must believe that He exists and that He is fully trustworthy. We must believe that God loves us. It's not possible to trust God if we don't believe what He says in His Word. God's actions and attention are directed on us because He loves us. God's love defines His deeds. Faith in God begins with an acceptance of His love.

Those who hope in the LORD will renew their strength. They will soar on wings like eagles; they will run and not grow weary, they will walk and not be faint.
Isaiah 40:31

I wait for the LORD, my whole being waits, and in His word I put my hope. I wait for the Lord more than watchmen wait for the morning, more that watchmen wait for the morning.
Psalm 130:5-6

THE PROCESS OF TRUST

To believe that God loves us is an important step in the process of faith and trust in God because it shows that we believe what God says. It is impossible to trust God if we don't believe what He says. From here trust develops into the belief that God loves us, His Word is true and that He will protect and guide us even in the worst possible circumstances. Trusting God is the key to fulfillment in our lives.

"Surely this is our God; we trusted in Him, and He saved us. This is the Lord, we trusted in Him; let us rejoice and be glad in His salvation."
Isaiah 25:9

"Though the mountains be shaken and the hills be removed, yet My unfailing love for you will not be shaken nor My covenant of peace be removed," says the Lord, who has compassion on you.
Isaiah 54:10

TRUST GOD WITH ALL YOUR BEING

Jesus is a safe harbor and He gives us victory over the things from which we want to flee. When overwhelming feelings of rejection and lovelessness encircle us, He is the One who rescues us and enables us to walk on the heights. We receive grace to wonderfully soar above our circumstances. God holds us safe, and to be safe is to feel good. Stay focused on God and trust Him with your whole being.

> *The Sovereign LORD is my strength;*
> *He makes my feet like the feet of a deer,*
> *He enables me to tread on the heights.*
> Habakkuk 3:19

> *God is our refuge and strength, an*
> *ever-present help in trouble. Therefore we*
> *will not fear, though the earth give way and*
> *the mountains fall into the heart of the sea.*
> Psalm 46:1-2

LOYAL TO JESUS

People often choose their church over Jesus. This sounds so terrible, but it is true. Many congregations exist for years without having Jesus in their midst. What they don't realize is that being connected to Jesus brings life and glory. We must love the Lord Jesus so much that He doesn't doubt that we are more loyal to Him than our church.

Do your best to present yourself to God as one approved, a worker who does not need to be ashamed and who correctly handles the word of truth.
2 Timothy 2:15

Guard my life and rescue me; do not let me be put to shame, for I take refuge in You. May integrity and uprightness protect me, because my hope, Lord, is in You.
Psalm 25:20-21

REMAIN FAITHFUL TO GOD

In Revelation 6, believers stand around God's throne. They were murdered and persecuted for their faith, as are many Christians today. We think that God isn't going to do anything to these murderers because He is not going to judge them, but this is not true. God gives unbelievers a period of grace in which they have a chance to repent. But when this period is over, God will pour His judgment out on them. Stay faithful and true to Jesus, no matter what happens. Always trust in His Word.

They called out in a loud voice, "How long, Sovereign Lord, holy and true, until You judge the inhabitants of the earth and avenge our blood?" Then each of them was given a white robe, and they were told to wait a little longer, until the full number of their fellow servants, their brothers and sisters, were killed just as they had been.

Revelation 6:10-11

The Lord knows how to rescue the godly from trials and to hold the unrighteous for punishment on the day of judgment.

2 Peter 2:9

TRUE ENJOYMENT IN LIFE

We all know the excitement and power that sport holds. For some people sport means more to them than God. It fills their life and gives meaning to their existence. This is more than sport is supposed to do.

There is nothing wrong with enjoying sport, but watch out that it doesn't take the place that only God can fill. Enjoy sport, but worship God. Always be loyal to Jesus – this is true life.

Therefore I do not run like someone running aimlessly;
I do not fight like a boxer beating the air.
1 Corinthians 9:26

"If you are faithful in little things, you will be faithful
in large ones. But if you are dishonest in little things,
you won't be honest with greater responsibilities."
Luke 16:10 NLT

FAITH IN JESUS

To believe in Jesus is to accept who He says He is – nothing less. We know that Jesus is the Supreme Authority of heaven and earth and that His sovereignty guarantees us eternal life.

Our comprehension of Jesus and faith in Him is visible and we lay our lives down before Him, trusting Him to rule over us as He thinks fit. We give Him unlimited access to our innermost being. This is the only faith that qualifies before God and that will gain His favor and open life in God for us.

Now faith is confidence in what we hope for
and assurance about what we do not see.
Hebrews 11:1

Jesus answered, "The work of God is this:
to believe in the one He has sent."
John 6:29

THE KEY TO LIFE

Faith in Jesus is a vital key to life. It means more than accepting your church's doctrine. Jesus is the way, the truth and the life. He is able to save us from death and to keep watch over our souls. He leads us to the heart of God despite the circumstances we find ourselves in. Faith in Jesus is the key to life in God.

Jesus said to her, "I am the resurrection and the life. The one who believes in Me will live, even though they die."
John 11:25

In the gospel the righteousness of God is revealed – a righteousness that is by faith from first to last, just as it is written: "The righteous will live by faith."
Romans 1:17

We live by faith, not by sight.
2 Corinthians 5:6-7

IS THERE HOPE?

When we yearn for hope, we yearn for life, prosperity, relief, peace, love, stability and reconciliation. The absence of hope strips us of a zest for life. There *is* hope, but it is only available in God. If we hope that nothing terrible will ever happen, our expectations are weak. But if we trust in God even when bad things happen, we have a firm anchor for our soul.

> *Be strong and take heart, all you*
> *who hope in the Lord.*
> Psalm 31:24

> *"Blessed is the one who trusts in the Lord,*
> *whose confidence is in Him."*
> Jeremiah 17:7

> *Blessed are those whose help is the God of Jacob,*
> *whose hope is in the Lord their God.*
> Psalm 146:5

GOD IS HOPE

Some situations seem hopeless from the start, but this doesn't mean that they are without hope. Even if we are thrown to the lions there is still hope – hope for life. God is our hope and this hope never shies away. Don't place your hope in people, but rather place your hope in the Man who died in your place on the cross of Calvary.

May the God of hope fill you with all joy and peace as you trust in Him, so that you may overflow with hope by the power of the Holy Spirit.
Romans 15:13

To them God has chosen to make known among the Gentiles the glorious riches of this mystery, which is Christ in you, the hope of glory.
Colossians 1:27

THE ONLY HOPE

The world's only hope is to be reconciled with God, but few people are prepared to drink from Jesus' cup of sorrow. The cost of following Jesus is to be unpopular with the world and few people are prepared to do this. It often boils down to Jesus being denied to keep the world happy. You can't share in Jesus' salvation without also sharing in His suffering. Ask Jesus to help you so that you don't swap Him for the world's mark of approval.

You adulterous people, don't you know that friendship with the world means enmity against God? Therefore, anyone who chooses to be a friend of the world becomes an enemy of God.

James 4:4

"I have given them Your word and the world has hated them, for they are not of the world any more than I am of the world. My prayer is not that You take them out of the world but that You protect them from the evil one."

John 17:14-15

YOU CAN'T COVER YOUR HEART

A lot can be said about what is an acceptable church dress code. Some say that you don't have to dress your best to go to church and others say that it's necessary to look smart.

There is more to the clothes debate than we care to admit. Deep in our hearts we know that we cannot appear before God because the light of His presence exposes all the unrighteousness in us. Our impurities force us to compensate when we have anything to do with God.

Ask God to purify you so that you can stand before Him without shame. It's not how you are dressed on the outside that counts, but what you look like on the inside.

The LORD said to Samuel, "Do not consider his appearance or his height, for I have rejected him. The LORD does not look at the things people look at. People look at the outward appearance, but the LORD looks at the heart."

1 Samuel 16:7

THE BEST DRESS

Instead of debating what we should wear to church we should focus on the heavenly wardrobe that is available to us through Jesus.

Isaiah says that one day we will be clothed in robes of righteousness. To be righteous means to be forgiven, purified and reconciled with God. Jesus is our righteousness and we look forward to our heavenly clothes that will never perish or fade.

I delight greatly in the LORD; my soul rejoices
in my God. For He has clothed me with garments of
salvation and arrayed me in a robe of His righteousness,
as a bridegroom adorns his head like a priest, and as
a bride adorns herself with her jewels.
Isaiah 61:10

The LORD rewards everyone for their
righteousness and faithfulness.
1 Samuel 26:23

A ROBE OF RIGHTEOUSNESS

The only Person who has unlimited access to the Father is Jesus Christ and the Father says that the only acceptable "clothes" to wear in His presence is Jesus Himself. Even a poor man with torn and dirty clothes can have a feast in God's presence if his heart is pure. Ask Jesus to clothe you in the robe of righteousness, without which you cannot stand before the Father.

Clothe yourself with the presence of the Lord Jesus Christ. And don't let yourself think about ways to indulge your evil desires.
Romans 13:14 NLT

Your beauty should not come from outward adornment, such as elaborate hairstyles and the wearing of gold jewelry or fine clothes. Rather, it should be that of your inner self, the unfading beauty of a gentle and quiet spirit, which is of great worth in God's sight.
1 Peter 3:3-4

PURE OF HEART

Purity of heart is the deepest and most important purity to God. Jesus says that those who are of pure heart will see God. A pure heart addresses the attitude of the heart. It's the manner in which we do things and the hidden motives and agendas behind our words and deeds. Ask God to give you a pure heart today.

"Blessed are the pure in heart, for they will see God."
Matthew 5:8

For the word of God is alive and active. Sharper than any double-edged sword, it penetrates even to dividing soul and spirit, joints and marrow; it judges the thoughts and attitudes of the heart.
Hebrews 4:12

Create in me a pure heart, O God, and renew a steadfast spirit within me.
Psalm 51:10

A HARD HEART

With hands lifted up and eyes shut we often stand before God with impure hearts. We have hearts that are unwilling to confess sin; they are hard and unwilling to honor and serve others. God doesn't politely request purity of heart, He demands it. If we bow our heart before God, His glory will overflow in our lives.

Nevertheless, the righteous will hold to their ways, and those with clean hands will grow stronger.

Job 17:9

Who may ascend the mountain of the LORD? Who may stand in His holy place? The one who has clean hands and a pure heart. They will receive blessing from the LORD and vindication from God their Savior.

Psalm 24:3-5

Flee the evil desires of youth and pursue righteousness, faith, love and peace, along with those who call on the Lord out of a pure heart.

2 Timothy 2:22

LONGING FOR A PURE HEART

Our soul desires to be pure. It's like when you spend a whole day in the hot sun and dust and then take a shower before supper. The relief to be clean again! It feels so good! This is also why we crave for purity in our soul. We are polluted and soiled with lies, rebellion and broken relationships and our soul longs to be clean. Ask Jesus to cleanse your heart and soul today.

Restore to me the joy of Your salvation and
grant me a willing spirit, to sustain me.
Psalm 51:12

"I will sprinkle clean water on you, and you
will be clean; I will cleanse you from all your
impurities and from all your idols."
Ezekiel 36:25

We know that when Christ appears, we shall be like
Him, for we shall see Him as He is. All who have
this hope in Him purify themselves,
just as He is pure.
1 John 3:2-3

PURITY OF SOUL

To have our soul cleansed and made pure removes all the baggage that we carry. We were created for purity, not uncleanliness. You know the sins that make you impure before God? Don't stew about them any longer. To be pure is within your reach. It is as close to you as Jesus. Lay it all before Jesus and let your soul rest in the knowledge that God has forgiven and purified you.

My soul faints with longing for Your salvation,
but I have put my hope in Your word.
Psalm 119:81

Therefore let us keep the Festival, not with the old
bread leavened with malice and wickedness, but
with the unleavened bread of sincerity and truth.
1 Corinthians 5:8

The goal of this command is love, which comes
from a pure heart and a good conscience
and a sincere faith.
1 Timothy 1:5

PURIFIED BY HIS WORD

God's Word purifies our heart. The Word of God is not about laws and regulations, but about a Person – Jesus Christ. He is the One who purifies our heart. To grow in Christ is to become pure. There is no other form of purity or way to become pure – only through God and His Word.

How can a young person stay on the path of purity?
By living according to Your word. I seek You
with all my heart; do not let me stray
from Your commands.
Psalm 119:9-10

The words of the LORD are flawless, like silver
purified in a crucible, like gold refined seven times.
Psalm 12:6

Now that you have purified yourselves by
obeying the truth so that you have sincere love
for each other, love one another deeply,
from the heart.
1 Peter 1:22

PURIFIED BUT NOT HEALED

The consequences of sin are like a long-standing illness. We can be forgiven and cleansed of sin, but still suffer the consequences many years later. This is a daily reality for many believers. Allow Jesus to heal you completely so that you no longer suffer the consequences of long-forgotten sins.

Present yourselves to God as being alive from the dead, and your members as instruments of righteousness to God. For sin shall not have dominion over you, for you are not under law but under grace.
Romans 6:13-14 NKJV

He heals the brokenhearted and binds up their wounds.
Psalm 147:3

INNER HEALING

The term "inner healing" refers to the healing of a person's heart from the pain of sin. The most powerful meetings we can have with Jesus has to do with healing the past. The problem is that we don't want to go back because the pain is too much. Jesus doesn't take people back to those terrible moments to traumatize them, but to bring about complete healing. Don't be afraid to trust God – allow Him to heal you from your past.

Therefore, if anyone is in Christ, the new creation
has come: The old has gone, the new is here!
2 Corinthians 5:17

On hearing this, Jesus said to them,
"It is not the healthy who need a doctor, but the sick.
I have not come to call the righteous, but sinners."
Mark 2:17

THE GREATEST HOPE

Most people are aware of the high walls that separate us. The world is so divided by race, religion, ethnic group, church, age group, rich and poor, learned and unschooled … it's basically never-ending. But Jesus breaks the dividing walls between man and man, and man and God. Jesus reconciles and reconstructs. To give yourself over to Him is to open yourself to forgiveness, reconciliation, recovery, healing, restitution and a healing of relationships. Herein lies the greatest hope for ourselves and for the world.

His purpose was to create in Himself one new humanity out of the two, thus making peace, and in one body to reconcile both of them to God through the cross, by which He put to death their hostility.
Ephesians 2:15-16

He Himself is our peace, who has made the two groups one and has destroyed the barrier, the dividing wall of hostility.
Ephesians 2:14

MAY

A CONSTANT COMPANION

If I ride the wings of the morning, if I dwell by the farthest oceans, even there Your hand will guide me, and Your strength will support me. Psalm 139:9-10 NLT

JESUS IS ALWAYS WITH US

Jesus is with us and He is in control. Trust that He is always with you. He wants to reveal Himself to you and He will. When doubt and anxiety grab hold of you, remember that Jesus is with you and that He is in charge. He is in control of your situation here and now; He has always been and will always be.

> *"The coming of the kingdom of God is not something that can be observed, nor will people say, 'Here it is,' or 'There it is,' because the kingdom of God is in your midst."*
>
> Luke 17:20-21

> *I know the LORD is always with me. I will not be shaken, for He is right beside me. No wonder my heart is glad, and I rejoice. My body rests in safety.*
>
> Psalm 16:8-9 NLT

WHERE IS GOD?

Some people try to make sense of suffering by saying that it is God's will and we should leave it at that. That's not true – God didn't create us to suffer. Suffering is a consequence of the sin man commits. God isn't left powerless through our misery. He is able to pick us up and save us from destruction, even when everything is falling apart. When you become despondent with all the devastation and death around you, praise God for the life He gives.

"Whoever lives by believing in Me will never die.
Do you believe this?"
John 11:26

"Have I not commanded you? Be strong and courageous.
Do not be afraid; do not be discouraged, for the LORD
your God will be with you wherever you go."
Joshua 1:9

INFINITE HOPE

Can God prevent people from suffering? Yes, He can and He does. God mercifully spares us from some of the suffering that comes our way and does not expose us to all of it. Jesus made the blind to see and the lame to walk. He raised people from the dead, reunited children with their parents and set the demon-possessed free. But more than this, He has placed in everyone who bows the knee to Him, the supernatural ability of possessing infinite hope and eternal life, even though they may be knocked down or even killed.

We are hunted down, but never abandoned by God. We get knocked down, but we are not destroyed.
2 Corinthians 4:9 NLT

Jesus replied, "Anyone who loves Me will obey My teaching. My Father will love them, and We will come to them and make Our home with them."
John 14:23

NEVER APATHETIC TO HUMAN SUFFERING

People in pain often become aggressive, especially towards God. God is never apathetic towards people: He became human and suffered under the hand of man in order to free us from sin and the devil – from all forms of suffering.

The Word became flesh and made His dwelling among us.
We have seen His glory, the glory of the one and only Son,
who came from the Father, full of grace and truth.

John 1:14

"I will be your God throughout your lifetime –
until your hair is white with age.
I made you, and I will care for you.
I will carry you along and save you."

Isaiah 46:4 NLT

COMPASSION FOR ALL PEOPLE

The Bible tells us that Jesus felt sorry for people because they were like sheep without a shepherd (Matthew 9:36), sick (Matthew 14:14), without food (Mark 8:2) and grieving lost loved ones (Luke 7:13).

Ask the Lord Jesus to help you not to be apathetic towards Him – especially after all He has done to free you from suffering.

The LORD is with you when you are with Him. If you seek Him, He will be found by you, but if you forsake Him, He will forsake you.
2 Chronicles 15:2

"You will seek Me and find Me when you seek Me with all your heart."
Jeremiah 29:13

As God's chosen people, holy and dearly loved, clothe yourselves with compassion.
Colossians 3:12

SUFFERING FOR CHRIST

Believers don't suffer because they have broken the law. To suffer for doing good and to continue to do good reveals the Spirit of God. It isn't God's will that anyone should do wrong – it never is. However, we live in a world dictated by darkness. It does not love the light because the light exposes the darkness. If we choose to dwell in the darkness, the Light, Jesus, cannot be our constant companion.

So then, those who suffer according to God's will should commit themselves to their faithful Creator and continue to do good.
1 Peter 4:19

Everyone who wants to live a godly life in Christ Jesus will suffer persecution.
2 Timothy 3:12 NLT

DARKNESS MAKES AN OFFER

In your life as a disciple of Christ there will be moments and situations where you are tempted to make a deal with darkness. Your family may turn against you and your friends distance themselves from you.

Even though you appear brave, these things strike like arrows deep within your heart. Then darkness plays its hand: "Forsake your relationship with Jesus and your life will return to normal." To sacrifice your relationship with Jesus for acceptance by others is catastrophic. Never accept the offer of darkness; turn back towards the Light.

"What do you benefit if you gain the whole world but lose your own soul? Is anything worth more than your soul?"
Matthew 16:26 NLT

It is for freedom that Christ has set us free. Stand firm, then, and do not let yourselves be burdened again by a yoke of slavery.
Galatians 5:1

THE GREATEST GAIN

To be a disciple of Christ, you need to put off your self. This concept is beautifully illustrated by suffering. To be accepted by others is a strong desire in us. People do things they don't even like in order to fit into a group.

To give up your popularity or acceptance by others in order to follow Jesus is very difficult for many believers. Even so, we mustn't be like Esau who gave up his birthright for a bowl of stew. Your gain is your priceless relationship with Jesus.

> *"Whoever does not carry their cross and follow Me cannot be My disciple."*
> Luke 14:27

> *Dear friends, do not be surprised at the fiery ordeal that has come on you to test you, as though something strange were happening to you. But rejoice inasmuch as you participate in the sufferings of Christ, so that you may be overjoyed when His glory is revealed.*
> 1 Peter 4:12-13

GOD WANTS ME TO SUFFER?

Firstly, God doesn't want us to suffer. It's a half-truth, and half-truths are dangerous. God does not rejoice in our sufferings. If He did, He wouldn't have sent Jesus to die in order to stop us from suffering due to our disobedience.

God is love. He is our Savior. He does not leave us to suffer in disobedience, but saves us. When we suffer for His sake, for doing good, we must realize that this is the suffering we should rejoice in and with which He is pleased.

Consider it pure joy, my brothers and sisters,
whenever you face trials of many kinds, because
you know that the testing of your faith
produces perseverance.
James 1:2-3

It is better, if it is God's will, to suffer
for doing good than for doing evil.
1 Peter 3:17

GOD HIMSELF IS THE REWARD

When people treat us unfairly and deny us our basic rights and privileges, unholy thoughts and behavior arise in us. We react childishly or vengefully. God wants us to recognize these things so that we can place them at Jesus' feet and be done with them. The flesh sucks God's life out of us. To be as pure and as clean as God is, is His will for our lives. The reward for our sacrifices is God Himself. There is no greater prize.

Do not forget to do good and to share with others,
for with such sacrifices God is pleased.
Hebrews 13:16

I urge you, brothers and sisters, in view of God's
mercy, to offer your bodies as a living sacrifice, holy and
pleasing to God – this is your true and proper worship.
Do not conform to the pattern of this world, but be
transformed by the renewing of your mind. Then you
will be able to test and approve what God's will is –
His good, pleasing and perfect will.
Romans 12:1-2

JESUS WALKS TOWARDS US

The crises that we face are channels through which Jesus reveals Himself. He comes, as it were, walking towards us in our crisis. The disciples experienced this when their boat was about to sink in the storm. The raging waters were their crisis. Then Jesus came towards them, walking on the water. He was in a place they never expected Him, doing something they never knew He could do. It was their perilous state that was the channel for Jesus to reveal Himself to them.

"When you go through deep waters, I will be with you. When you go through rivers of difficulty, you will not drown. When you walk through the fire of oppression, you will not be burned up; the flames will not consume you. For I am the LORD, your God, the Holy One of Israel, your Savior."

Isaiah 43:2-3 NLT

The God of all grace, who called you to His eternal glory in Christ, after you have suffered a little while, will Himself restore you and make you strong, firm and steadfast.

1 Peter 5:10

JESUS IN THE CRISIS

When we try to avoid a crisis by fleeing from it, we lose an opportunity for Jesus to reveal Himself to us. We don't expect Jesus in the crises in our lives, blaming it on the devil instead. We don't realize that the crisis could be one of the greatest breakthroughs in our lives. Take another look at your crisis – the solution and glory you seek is to be found in Jesus in the crisis.

Blessed is the one who perseveres under trial
because, having stood the test, that person will
receive the crown of life that the Lord has
promised to those who love Him.
James 1:12

We also glory in our sufferings,
because we know that suffering produces
perseverance; perseverance, character; and
character, hope. And hope does not put us to shame,
because God's love has been poured out into our hearts
through the Holy Spirit, who has been given to us.
Romans 5:3-5

DON'T PUSH YOUR CRISIS AWAY

It is not easy to see Jesus in our crisis. It is also not so easy to get into the practice of drawing our crises closer. It's something we have to remind each other of continually.

To embrace our crisis is to allow Jesus to cleanse us and rebuild us in areas that don't normally receive attention. This is when the great channels of God's grace are opened. Then the crises that were first our boss become our servants. Jesus is now in control!

In my desperation I prayed, and the LORD listened;
He saved me from all my troubles.
Psalm 34:6 NLT

"I have told you these things, so that in Me you may
have peace. In this world you will have trouble.
But take heart! I have overcome the world."
John 16:33

JESUS AND STORMS

The manner in which God works is so different from the way of the world. God's focus is on His Son, Jesus Christ – the expression and definition of God's character and Person.

In Jesus is the fullness of the Godhead and all the answers and solutions we will ever need. The key to peace in a crisis is the Person of Jesus Christ. If there are great storms in your life and anxiety is pulling you under, ask God to reveal Himself to you. He will give you the greatest peace in the midst of the storm.

In Him dwells all the fullness of the Godhead bodily; and you are complete in Him, who is the head of all principality and power.
Colossians 2:9-10 NKJV

He got up, rebuked the wind and said to the waves, "Quiet! Be still!" Then the wind died down and it was completely calm. He said to His disciples, "Why are you so afraid? Do you still have no faith?"
Mark 4:39-40

OVERCOME YOUR FEAR

Fear is part of being human. Some people are bound by the same fear for many years and can't seem to break free. Was Jesus ever afraid? Yes, He was. In the Garden of Gethsemane, Jesus was afraid of what lay ahead of Him. Yet, He knew that the Father, even in the midst of the gruesome event that lay ahead, was still God and He placed Himself totally into His hands. This was the victory over the fear of the cross. Jesus was totally human and faced the same things we do, but He overcame. We can also overcome fear by placing it in the Father's hands.

Even when I walk through the darkest valley,
I will not be afraid, for You are close beside me.
Your rod and Your staff protect and comfort me.
Psalm 23:4 NLT

"I am the LORD *your God who takes*
hold of your right hand and says to you,
Do not fear; I will help you."
Isaiah 41:13

JESUS, THE GREATEST PROBLEM SOLVER

We face problems every day. We can flee from them or fight against them, or we can solve them. Jesus proves that He is capable and willing to help us in every problem we face. Through our problems Jesus shows us who He really is and that He will do the things He says He will do. Let Jesus be your companion through life and you will experience His help through the problems that come upon your path.

"Come to Me, all you who are weary and burdened, and I will give you rest. Take My yoke upon you and learn from Me, for I am gentle and humble in heart, and you will find rest for your souls. For My yoke is easy and My burden is light."

Matthew 11:28-30

The disciples saw Jesus do many other miraculous signs in addition to the ones recorded in this book. But these are written so that you may continue to believe that Jesus is the Messiah, the Son of God, and that by believing in Him you will have life by the power of His name.

John 20:30-31 NLT

GRACE IN TROUBLED TIMES

Our world and our character are shaped by problems and difficulties. Stumbling blocks shape our perspective and even our image of God. Working through difficulties gives us the privilege of experiencing God in a way that is otherwise not possible this side of the grave. Ask the Lord Jesus to reveal to you how His grace is sufficient for all the troubles and problems you might face.

"My grace is sufficient for you, for My power is made perfect in weakness." Therefore I will boast all the more gladly about my weaknesses, so that Christ's power may rest on me.

2 Corinthians 12:9

I consider that our present sufferings are not worth comparing with the glory that will be revealed in us.

Romans 8:18

JESUS IS THE ANSWER!

Some people accuse Jesus of self-aggrandizement when He says that He is the only way to the Father. This of course is nothing short of blasphemy. It is a fact that whether people accept it or not, Jesus brings about the greatest crisis in our lives – the crisis between life and death. Ask Jesus to reveal to you whether you are resisting Him or embracing Him so that He can be the true and only solution in your life.

Jesus answered, "I am the way and the truth and the life. No one comes to the Father except through Me. If you really know Me, you will know My Father as well."
John 14:6-7

"Do not suppose that I have come to bring peace to the earth. I did not come to bring peace, but a sword."
Matthew 10:34

THE WAY TO END CONFLICT

In the first reference that God makes to the Savior that He is going to send to mankind (Genesis 3:15), God reveals that this Savior will be involved in conflict. Jesus brings conflict and crises, yet He is God's solution to the brokenness in the world. Choose today to make Jesus the solution to the conflict in your life.

"Do you think I came to bring peace on earth?
No, I tell you, but division."
Luke 12:51

Now listen! Today I am giving you a choice between
life and death, between prosperity and disaster. For I
command you this day to love the LORD your God
and to keep His commands, decrees, and regulations
by walking in His ways. If you do this, you will live
and multiply, and the LORD your God will bless you
and the land you are about to enter and occupy.
Deuteronomy 30:15-16 NLT

CHOOSE LIFE

Jesus is the way to life. He not only gives us life "one day when we die," but also here and now. The life that we need is to have a meaningful existence, to live free from the power of sin and to be able to have a relationship with God. All this comes from the life we have in Jesus Christ. Choose Jesus today and you will have glorious life from now into eternity.

The wages of sin is death, but the gift of God is eternal life in Christ Jesus our Lord.
Romans 6:23

This day I call the heavens and the earth as witnesses against you that I have set before you life and death, blessings and curses. Now choose life, so that you and your children may live.
Deuteronomy 30:19

SURRENDER TO JESUS

Before we give our lives to Jesus, we often experience a crisis in our hearts. There is a conflict between choosing Jesus or living for the self. This choice could ultimately result in death.

Once we stop fighting and surrender our heart to Jesus, we experience true life. We can only truly become victors when we join the Lord's side and allow Him to reign in our hearts.

The Lord your God will circumcise your hearts
and the hearts of your descendants, so that you
may love Him with all your heart and
with all your soul, and live.
Deuteronomy 30:6

To this you were called, because Christ
suffered for you, leaving you an example,
that you should follow in His steps.
1 Peter 2:21

JESUS IS THE PRIZE

When we surrender our hearts to Jesus, we must make sure that the flesh does not take over again. Ask God to help you to do His will, and desire to please Him. As soon as you realize that the world has nothing to offer, you will realize that Jesus is the true and greatest prize. He is your heart's crown of great beauty.

"'If you can'?" said Jesus. "Everything is possible
for one who believes." Immediately the boy's father
exclaimed, "I do believe; help me overcome my unbelief!"
Mark 9:23-24

Teach me knowledge and good judgment,
for I trust Your commands. Before I was
afflicted I went astray, but now I obey Your word.
Psalm 119:66-67

DON'T GIVE IN!

When we are faced with temptation we experience a crisis between good and evil in our hearts. We desire to please God but there is a strong fleshly desire to do wrong. At times such as this, pray to God to help you. Tell Him that you are weak and that you stumble. Ask Him to strengthen you to resist evil.

Do not throw away your confidence; it will be richly rewarded. You need to persevere so that when you have done the will of God, you will receive what He has promised.
Hebrews 10:35-36

Therefore, since we are surrounded by such a great cloud of witnesses, let us throw off everything that hinders and the sin that so easily entangles. And let us run with perseverance the race marked out for us.
Hebrews 12:1

BETWEEN THE DEVIL AND THE DEEP BLUE SEA

When someone is facing a terrible dilemma we say that they are between the devil and the deep blue sea. This implies that they can choose between hell and the depths of the sea. Not much of a choice! But is this saying really true? I don't think so. There is another choice for disciples of Jesus. Next time you find yourself between the devil and the deep blue sea, reach out to Jesus. He has already conquered the devil and He created the mighty depths of the sea! Nothing is too great for Him.

Praise the LORD. Blessed are those who fear the LORD, who find great delight in His commands.
Psalm 112:1

Blessed is the one who does not walk in step with the wicked or stand in the way that sinners take or sit in the company of mockers, but whose delight is in the law of the Lord, and who meditates on His law day and night.
Psalm 1:1-2

FLEE TO JESUS

We can flee to any place to escape our problems and fears, yet we flee so seldom to Jesus. Many people only run into Jesus' safe arms when they've already tried all the other options.

It is unnecessary for believers to get into a state of panic when a crisis hits them. Run to Jesus and trust that He is in control when you no longer are. You will experience peace instead of panic.

"Can anyone hide from Me in a secret place?
Am I not everywhere in all the heavens and earth?"
says the LORD.
Jeremiah 23:24 NLT

Be my rock of refuge, to which I can always go;
give the command to save me, for You are my
rock and my fortress.
Psalm 71:3

FLEE TO YOUR HELPER

When you flee to Jesus, He fights your battle for you and helps you to overcome. In this case it is not cowardly to flee, but wise. God helps us to be victorious when on our own we would not be able to overcome our problems.

We cannot fight all our battles on our own. Our strength lies in fleeing to Jesus, the great overcomer. Are you tired of fighting; have you been wounded in battle? Then it is time to flee. Flee to Jesus. He will help you to fight your battle and be victorious.

He is my loving ally and my fortress, my tower of safety, my rescuer. He is my shield, and I take refuge in Him.
Psalm 144:2 NLT

God is our refuge and strength, an ever-present help in trouble. Therefore we will not fear, though the earth give way and the mountains fall into the heart of the sea, though its waters roar and foam and the mountains quake with their surging.
Psalm 46:1-3

RUN IN THE RIGHT DIRECTION

We flee to Jesus to escape unrighteousness. We must guard against just running away from unrighteousness and not running to Jesus. If we don't run to Jesus, unrighteousness will inevitably catch up with us. Jesus is the only place where you are guaranteed to feel safe and free.

But you, flee from all this, and pursue righteousness, godliness, faith, love, endurance and gentleness. Fight the good fight of the faith. Take hold of the eternal life to which you were called when you made your good confession in the presence of many witnesses.

1 Timothy 6:11-12

Run from anything that stimulates youthful lusts. Instead, pursue righteous living, faithfulness, love, and peace. Enjoy the companionship of those who call on the Lord with pure hearts.

2 Timothy 2:22 NLT

THE SOURCE OF COURAGE

Jesus will always be in the presence of His disciples, even though He is not physically present. They might appear to be alone, but they are definitely not by themselves. God's Spirit is always with them. The Holy Spirit, the Comforter, will establish the authority and peace of Christ. Jesus' disciples can be assured of His presence with them. This gives us courage: We never have to walk alone.

"I will ask the Father, and He will give you another Advocate, who will never leave you."
John 14:16 NLT

You who are my Comforter in sorrow, my heart is faint within me.
Jeremiah 8:18

The Lord replied, "My Presence will go with you, and I will give you rest."
Exodus 33:14

WHY DO I HAVE TO SUFFER?

We might ask why, even when we are walking with God, we experience difficulties. Why don't we have an advantage over unbelievers and be spared from suffering because God is our Father? We look at unbelievers who are super-successful and free from problems and think it's not fair.

The fact is that hard times can hit anyone, regardless of who they are. Instead of moaning about how unfair your problems are, roll up your sleeves and get to work and keep your eyes focused on the glory of God. He will help you through.

Whatever you do, work at it with all your heart,
as working for the Lord, not for human masters,
since you know that you will receive an inheritance
from the Lord as a reward. It is the
Lord Christ you are serving.
Colossians 3:23-24

Commit to the LORD whatever you do,
and He will establish your plans.
Proverbs 16:3

WHAT IS SUCCESS?

The world looks at successful people and thinks they have it all. But what is true success? Health is not the greatest profit because you can lose it so easily. Success does not lie in your possessions, wealth or standard of living because they are all temporary. Our success lies in having God in our lives.

Our most valuable possession is Jesus Christ in our hearts. All else will fade away, but an intimate relationship with God will last forever.

Take delight in the LORD, and He will give you the desires of your heart.
Psalm 37:4

He will fulfill the desire of those who fear Him; He also will hear their cry and save them.
Psalm 145:19 NKJV

THE KEY TO A SUCCESSFUL LIFE

As we think about the fleetingness of worldly success, it is a direct comparison to how stable Jesus is. The key to true success is to have Jesus as your constant companion. Hardships and difficulties may come, but as you walk with your hand in His, you will be able to weather any storm that comes your way.

Jesus Christ is the same yesterday and today and forever.
Hebrews 13:8

Truly He is my rock and my salvation; He is my fortress, I will not be shaken. My salvation and my honor depend on God; He is my mighty rock, my refuge.
Psalm 62:6-7

JUNE

PRAISE TO THE LORD, THE ALMIGHTY, THE KING OF CREATION

The sea is His, for He made it, and His hands formed the dry land. Come, let us bow down in worship, let us kneel before the Lord our Maker. Psalm 95:5-6

PRAISE GOD FOR BEARING THE CURSE

The Jewish leaders crucified Jesus because they believed that anyone who was hung on a tree was cursed (see Deuteronomy 21:23). In their malice they completely lost sight of the fact that it was God's plan – that the curse we should have received was put on Jesus. Praise and thank the Lord that He became a curse for you so that you yourself did not have to be cursed.

God demonstrates His own love for us in this:
While we were still sinners,
Christ died for us.
Romans 5:8

He is the atoning sacrifice for our sins, and not
only for ours but also for the sins of
the whole world.
1 John 2:2

AN INDESCRIBABLE GIFT

When Jesus suffered on the cross, He fully and completely took upon Himself the punishment that was due to us. He was judged so that we do not need to be judged. He was raised from the dead so that we can be raised along with Him. Praise the Lord for the wonderful gift of life through Him.

Christ also suffered once for sins, the righteous for the unrighteous, to bring you to God. He was put to death in the body but made alive in the Spirit.
1 Peter 3:18

He was pierced for our transgressions, He was crushed for our iniquities; the punishment that brought us peace was on Him, and by His wounds we are healed.
Isaiah 53:5

REJOICE BECAUSE GOD REJOICES IN YOU

In God there is joy and peace, consideration, empathy and good fruit. Jesus is filled with joy because the Father is joyful. The Father rejoices and celebrates. He rejoices over us with singing. May you be filled with joy at the thought that God rejoices over you.

The LORD your God is living among you. He is a mighty savior. He will take delight in you with gladness. With His love, He will calm all your fears. He will rejoice over you with joyful songs."
Zephaniah 3:17 NLT

The wisdom that comes from heaven is first of all pure; then peace-loving, considerate, submissive, full of mercy and good fruit, impartial and sincere.
James 3:17

PRAISE GOD FOR HIS WONDERFUL CREATION

Meditate on the following verses today and praise God for His creation, for each new day and for the life He gives us.

You make known to me the path of life; You will fill me with joy in Your presence, with eternal pleasures at Your right hand.

Psalm 16:11

The whole earth is filled with awe at Your wonders; where morning dawns, where evening fades, You call forth songs of joy.

Psalm 65:8

Praise the Lord from the heavens; praise Him in the heights above. Praise Him, all His angels; praise Him, all His heavenly hosts. Praise Him, sun and moon; praise Him, all you shining stars. Praise Him, you highest heavens and you waters above the skies. Let them praise the name of the Lord, for at His command they were created.

Psalm 148:1-5

ENTHUSIASTIC ABOUT GOD

The Father loves His Son and makes known His pleasure and joy in Him. We can share in this enthusiasm about Jesus. Don't be embarrassed about Jesus or by those who unashamedly show their love for Him. Remain in His light until the dawn breaks and the morning star arises in your heart.

We also have the prophetic message as something completely reliable, and you will do well to pay attention to it, as to a light shining in a dark place, until the day dawns and the morning star rises in your hearts.
2 Peter 1:19

He received honor and glory from God the Father when the voice came to Him from the Majestic Glory, saying, "This is My Son, whom I love; with Him I am well pleased."
2 Peter 1:17

IT'S OK TO LAUGH

For centuries some churches have believed that the more serious you are, the closer you are to God. To laugh exuberantly was considered carnal. How surprising to find that God can laugh and rejoice. God delights in people and is involved in their lives. There is much more to following Jesus than wearing the right church clothes and having the fanciest church building. Praise the Lord for that!

Great is the LORD and most worthy of praise;
He is to be feared above all gods.
1 Chronicles 16:25

Sing and make music from your heart to the
Lord, always giving thanks to God the Father for
everything, in the name of our Lord Jesus Christ.
Ephesians 5:19-20

WHO YOU ARE IN CHRIST

One of life's great questions is "Who am I?" We are all on a personal voyage of discovery that begins at birth and ends when we die. We hope to discover that we make a meaningful contribution to society and the world around us.

The wonderful thing about this journey is that we discover God along the way and realize that He has a plan and purpose for our lives. Life is an amazing adventure in which we face difficult times, but we can always find the courage to continue through God's glory. Thank the Father for this wonderful adventure!

"I know the plans I have for you," declares the
LORD, "plans to prosper you and not to harm
you, plans to give you hope and a future."
Jeremiah 29:11

The Lord says, "I will instruct you and teach you in
the way you should go; I will counsel you with
My loving eye on you."
Psalm 32:8

HONOR GOD

To live honorably is very important to us. God created us to desire this and there is much value in honorable things. God's character is the essence of all that is honorable. The Holy Spirit teaches this to every disciple of Jesus Christ.

God's definition of honor is not a striving towards the great things in life, but faithfulness in the simple, everyday things. It means that we don't need special gifts to be honorable – we need God. To live an honorable life is to honor God.

Fear the LORD your God, serve Him only and take your oaths in His name.
Deuteronomy 6:13

Fear the LORD your God and serve Him. Hold fast to Him and take your oaths in His name.
Deuteronomy 10:20

A LIVING RELATIONSHIP

You cannot negotiate with God on matters such as salvation. However, there are issues that you can bring before God and questions that you can ask Him. God has not created us as robots. We are able to discuss matters with Him in prayer and He will listen to us with love and respect. Praise God for the living and loving relationship that we are able to have with Him.

Therefore, "Come out from them and be separate, says the Lord. Touch no unclean thing, and I will receive you." And, "I will be a Father to you, and you will be My sons and daughters, says the Lord Almighty."
2 Corinthians 6:17-18

We are co-workers in God's service; you are God's field, God's building.
1 Corinthians 3:9

TALKING TO GOD

Many people pray, "Your will be done …" This is good and proper, but it is incomplete because God still wants to work with us. He wants us to share our concerns and questions with Him. This doesn't mean that God has to do what we ask, but He cares about us and is willing to listen to what we have to say. As a believer you are in a relationship with God, so talk to Him. Praise Him for who He is and what He does for you.

The eyes of the Lord are on the righteous and His ears are attentive to their prayer, but the face of the Lord is against those who do evil.
1 Peter 3:12

Is anyone among you in trouble? Let them pray. Is anyone happy? Let them sing songs of praise.
James 5:13

INVISIBLE JESUS

When we talk to someone we want them to look at us so that we can see that they are listening. How do you talk to Jesus then if you can't see Him? Through the Holy Spirit we know that our perceptions concern spiritual and non-material things. This kind of perception is only possible for those who have been born again and have had their spiritual eyes opened by God. He gives us the ability to see and experience Him even in the darkest of circumstances. Praise Him for His presence even though we cannot physically see Him.

The person without the Spirit does not accept the things that come from the Spirit of God but considers them foolishness, and cannot understand them because they are discerned only through the Spirit.

1 Corinthians 2:14

"I will ask the Father, and He will give you another advocate to help you and be with you forever – the Spirit of truth. The world cannot accept Him, because it neither sees Him nor knows Him. But you know Him, for He lives with you and will be in you."

John 14:16-17

A WONDERFUL PRIVILEGE

To hear Jesus' voice is one of the privileges of being born again and it is the critical ingredient of a relationship with God. It doesn't mean that you can hear everything crystal clear and understand everything perfectly. As new believers we need more mature believers to help us discern what God is saying to us. Praise God for the wonderful privilege of hearing and recognizing His voice.

"I am the good shepherd; I know My sheep and My sheep know Me – just as the Father knows Me and I know the Father – and I lay down My life for the sheep. I have other sheep that are not of this sheep pen. I must bring them also. They too will listen to My voice, and there shall be one flock and one shepherd."

John 10:14-16

Listen! Listen to the roar of His voice, to the rumbling that comes from His mouth.

Job 37:2

WILLING TO LISTEN

We learn to recognize God's voice in various ways. One way is to learn from fellow believers who have a more mature relationship with God. Another way is to be obedient to what God is telling you to do. God speaks to those that are willing to do His will. Do what God is asking of you and you will hear His voice.

This is what the Lord says, He who made the earth, the Lord who formed it and established it – the Lord is His name: "Call to Me and I will answer you and tell you great and unsearchable things you do not know."
Jeremiah 33:2-3

"Whoever has ears, let them hear what the Spirit says to the churches."
Revelation 3:22

HEARING GOD'S VOICE

You need to want to hear God's voice. To read the Bible and meditate on what it says is one way of desiring to hear God's voice. Making time to speak to Him is another way. It is amazing how easy it actually is to hear God speak. All we have to do is to be willing to listen. Praise God for His willingness to speak to us.

*I will listen to what God the LORD says; He promises
peace to His people, His faithful servants – but let
them not turn to folly. Surely His salvation is near
those who fear Him, that His glory
may dwell in our land.*

Psalm 85:8-9

*In the morning, LORD, You hear my voice;
in the morning I lay my requests before You
and wait expectantly.*

Psalm 5:3

JESUS SPEAKS TO US

God wants to speak to us. When we are born again, God opens our spiritual ears so that we can hear what He wants to tell us. God loves to communicate with His children. To be able to hear God's voice is not something reserved for the super-spiritual, but for every child of God.

Jesus answered, "My teaching is not My own. It comes from the One who sent Me. Anyone who chooses to do the will of God will find out whether My teaching comes from God or whether I speak on My own."
John 7:16-17

"Whoever belongs to God hears what God says. The reason you do not hear is that you do not belong to God."
John 8:47

UNANSWERED PRAYER

All disciples of Jesus at one or other time find that Jesus says no to a request or doesn't seem to answer at all. What do you do when Jesus does not answer your prayers? The question you then need to ask is whether Jesus is still your Lord and God even though He doesn't answer your prayers. The greatest breakthrough in your life will come when you decide to worship God even though your prayers are not answered in the way you would like. Jesus is unconditionally yours and you are unconditionally His.

"You will be silent and not able to speak until the day this happens, because you did not believe my words, which will come true at their appointed time."
Luke 1:20

We know that God does not listen to sinners. He listens to the godly person who does His will.
John 9:31

PRAISE GOD FOR HIS INFINITE LOVE

Isn't it amazing to think that God loves us, sinners that we are? God's love is unconditional and eternal. Praise Him today for His infinite love.

> *You are my God, and I will praise You; You are my God, and I will exalt You. Give thanks to the LORD, for He is good; His love endures forever.*
>
> Psalm 118:28-29

> *I am convinced that neither death nor life, neither angels nor demons, neither the present nor the future, nor any powers, neither height nor depth, nor anything else in all creation, will be able to separate us from the love of God that is in Christ Jesus our Lord.*
>
> Romans 8:38-39

> *The LORD appeared to us in the past, saying: "I have loved you with an everlasting love; I have drawn you with unfailing kindness."*
>
> Jeremiah 31:3

BE WILLING TO LISTEN

There are many things that God will not specifically answer because He has revealed them in His Word. To expect God to say something to you personally when it is already in the Bible is to ignore Him and rebel against Him. The Bible says that if you are willing and listen, you will eat of the fat of the land.

"If you are willing and obedient, you will eat the good things of the land; but if you resist and rebel, you will be devoured by the sword."
For the mouth of the Lord has spoken.
Isaiah 1:19-20

Consequently, faith comes from hearing the message, and the message is heard through the word about Christ.
Romans 10:17

GLORIFYING GOD THROUGH YOUR ACTIONS

To pray before a game or match means that we are talking to God. This is a good thing, but the question is why we do it and what we are asking of God. Some people are only interested in God for a win. To pray before a match or look heavenward when you score a goal doesn't mean much if you don't also serve God. A life that is dedicated to God does more to glorify Him than just winning a game.

Physical training is of some value, but godliness has value for all things, holding promise for both the present life and the life to come.
1 Timothy 4:8

I consider my life worth nothing to me; my only aim is to finish the race and complete the task the Lord Jesus has given me – the task of testifying to the good news of God's grace.
Acts 20:24

PRAISE GOD FOR HIS PROVISION

There are people who chase after things that don't really matter and neglect the things that do. People work long hours and spend days, weeks or even months away from home to make money, only to realize that the true riches in life are not to be found in money. It is not wrong to be rich, but rather be rich in the Lord and not in earthly possessions. Praise God for meeting your needs, whether you have much or little.

"I counsel you to buy from Me gold refined in the fire, so you can become rich; and white clothes to wear, so you can cover your shameful nakedness; and salve to put on your eyes, so you can see."

Revelation 3:18

These have come so that the proven genuineness of your faith – of greater worth than gold, which perishes even though refined by fire – may result in praise, glory and honor when Jesus Christ is revealed.

1 Peter 1:7

GRATITUDE BRINGS GLORY TO GOD

A lot has been said about thankfulness and a lot will still be said in the future. Why? This is a very important topic for disciples of Christ, because in gratitude lies the glorification of God. Thankfulness is a divine command. Thankful people testify that they see and experience God's goodness in everyday things. Praise God for His blessings, great and small!

*Give thanks in all circumstances; for this is God's
will for you in Christ Jesus.*
1 Thessalonians 5:18

*"Worthy is the Lamb, who was slain, to receive power
and wealth and wisdom and strength and honor
and glory and praise!"*
Revelation 5:12

*Give praise to the LORD, proclaim His name;
make known among the nations
what He has done.*
1 Chronicles 16:8

GOD'S BLESSINGS

Will God bless us if we give? No, God's blessings do not depend on how much we give. God blesses us if we are obedient. God doesn't sell blessings for cash. Giving money to our church does not mean that God will bless us one hundred fold. We must be obedient to receive God's blessings. We honor God and worship Him through giving – we don't give to receive.

*Jesus replied, "Blessed rather are those who hear
the word of God and obey it."*
Luke 11:28

*The Lord's curse is on the house of the wicked,
but He blesses the home of the righteous.
He mocks proud mockers but shows favor
to the humble and oppressed.*
Proverbs 3:33-34

PRAISE THE LORD!

Jesus Christ is God's main focus, joy and love. He is God's solution and answer to man's problems. He is the glory of God through the ages. Praise God that you have life and that you can take part in the salvation and redemption that Jesus brings.

"The sounds of joy and gladness, the voices of bride and bridegroom, and the voices of those who bring thank offerings to the house of the LORD, saying, 'Give thanks to the LORD Almighty, for the LORD is good; His love endures forever.' For I will restore the fortunes of the land as they were before," says the LORD.
Jeremiah 33:11

My mouth is filled with Your praise, declaring Your splendor all day long.
Psalm 71:8

GOD IS HOLY

The Lord Jesus cleanses us so that we can stand unashamed in God's presence. Because of Jesus, we can experience God's holiness. Bow your knee before God and praise Him for giving you access to His throne through Jesus Christ. Praise Him for forgiving your sins and cleansing you so that you can stand in His presence.

His anger lasts only a moment, but His favor lasts a
lifetime; weeping may stay for the night,
but rejoicing comes in the morning.
Psalm 30:5

They were calling to one another: "Holy, holy,
holy is the LORD Almighty; the whole
earth is full of His glory."
Isaiah 6:3

JESUS IS OUR CELEBRATION

God's love and grace give us a reason to celebrate Jesus every day of the year. The right way to celebrate Jesus is through a life that is dedicated to Him. We don't have to wait for Christmas to celebrate Jesus, because Jesus is our celebration! Praise and worship Him every day of the year, because He died for our sins so that we could have a new life. The feast of God never ends.

Rejoice in the Lord always. I will say it again: Rejoice!
Philippians 4:4

They tell of the power of Your awesome works – and I proclaim Your great deeds. They celebrate Your abundant goodness and joyfully sing of Your righteousness.
Psalm 145:6-7

CELEBRATE JESUS

Praise Jesus every day by accepting who He is. Accept His authority, status and position and submit yourself to Him so that you can truly celebrate Him. Jesus offers more than mere sentiment; He offers a changed life and reconciliation with God and others. Delight yourself in the Lord – that is the true feast!

Honor the LORD for the glory of His name. Worship the LORD in the splendor of His holiness. The voice of the LORD echoes above the sea. The God of glory thunders. The LORD thunders over the mighty sea.
Psalm 29:2-3 NLT

I will be glad and rejoice in You; I will sing the praises of Your name, O Most High.
Psalm 9:2

THE GLORY OF THE LORD

Jesus allows us to share in His glory. He allows us to stand in His glory before the Father. All we have to concern ourselves with is to love Him and enjoy Him. Praise the Lord for the life we can have in Him and that He fills our entire beings. This is true life!

"I have given them the glory that You gave Me, that they may be one as We are one – I in them and You in Me – so that they may be brought to complete unity."
John 17:22-23

We all, who with unveiled faces contemplate the Lord's glory, are being transformed into His image with ever-increasing glory, which comes from the Lord, who is the Spirit.
2 Corinthians 3:18

TRUE LIFE IN ABUNDANCE

There is a deep-seated emptiness within every person who has not been made right with God. This is because God created man to be in a relationship with Him. Man's purpose in life is only fully realized in his unity and relationship with God.

Let us praise and worship the Lord for revealing our life's purpose to us and giving us true life in abundance.

I will exalt You, LORD, for You lifted me out of the
depths and did not let my enemies gloat over me.
Psalm 30:1

Praise the LORD, my soul; all my inmost being,
praise His holy name. Praise the LORD, my
soul, and forget not all His benefits.
Psalm 103:1-2

PRAISE THE LORD OUR SAVIOR

The Father was ready to sacrifice His Son for our sins before the beginning of the world, even before sin was there to infect and destroy humankind. Not only did the Father create everything through Jesus, but He also had salvation prepared before sin even entered the world. Praise God for having a Savior ready before the world even existed.

Our God is a God who saves; from the Sovereign
LORD comes escape from death. Surely God will
crush the heads of His enemies, the hairy
crowns of those who go on in their sins.
Psalm 68:20-21

To the only God our Savior be glory, majesty,
power and authority, through Jesus Christ our
Lord, before all ages, now and forevermore! Amen.
Jude 25

WORSHIP THE HOLY AND ALMIGHTY GOD

Take time to meditate on the holiness and sovereignty of God. Praise Him for His greatness as you read these Scriptures.

Fear the LORD, you His holy people, for those who fear Him lack nothing. The lions may grow weak and hungry, but those who seek the LORD lack no good thing.
Psalm 34:9-10

Therefore, since we are receiving a kingdom that cannot be shaken, let us be thankful, and so worship God acceptably with reverence and awe.
Hebrews 12:28

Praise the name of the LORD, for His name alone is exalted; His splendor is above the earth and the heavens. And He has raised up for His people a horn, the praise of all His faithful servants, the people close to His heart. Praise the LORD.
Psalm 148:13-14

JULY

INTO THE DEPTHS OF THE SEA

Who is a God like You, who pardons sin and forgives the transgression of the remnant of His inheritance? You do not stay angry forever but delight to show mercy. You will again have compassion on us; You will tread our sins underfoot and hurl all our iniquities into the depths of the sea. Micah 7:18-19

IS GOD GRACIOUS?

God hates sin, and disobedience must be punished. But even within God's punishment there is mercy. He is with us even when we walk the road of punishment for sin. God is always with us, ready to reach out to us if we would only call to Him for salvation. Kneel before the Lord Jesus and praise Him for His endless love – even when we have been rebellious.

He saved us, not because of righteous things we had done, but because of His mercy. He saved us through the washing of rebirth and renewal by the Holy Spirit.

Titus 3:5

Because of the LORD's great love we are not consumed, for His compassions never fail. They are new every morning; great is Your faithfulness.

Lamentations 3:22-23

HEAVEN OR HELL?

Many people find it difficult to understand that our loving God is also a God that allows people to go to hell. It is important to realize that God doesn't force anyone to go to hell; people choose to go there when they choose to reject God.

God invites us to turn to Him for salvation and eternal life, but He leaves us to decide whether we will accept Him or not. God does not want anyone to perish, but He allows people to make their own choices. Do you choose heaven or hell?

"Do not be afraid of those who kill the body but cannot kill the soul. Rather, be afraid of the One who can destroy both soul and body in hell."
Matthew 10:28

Do not withhold Your mercy from me, LORD; may Your love and faithfulness always protect me.
Psalm 40:11

JESUS' ENEMIES

From Jesus' teachings about how to handle enemies, we learn how He does it. He blesses those who curse Him, does good to those who hate Him and prays for those who mock and persecute Him.

If God didn't treat us in the way He tells us to treat our enemies, there would be no hope or salvation for us. It is beneficial to know what God's attitude towards us is, even if we are still enemies of the Lord. It helps us to see how we need to walk in grace with others.

"I tell you, love your enemies and pray for those who persecute you, that you may be children of your Father in heaven. He causes His sun to rise on the evil and the good, and sends rain on the righteous and the unrighteous."

Matthew 5:44-45

Once you were alienated from God and were enemies in your minds because of your evil behavior.

Colossians 1:21

BAD PEOPLE NEVER GET BURIED

Have you ever heard it said that bad people never get buried? It doesn't matter how bad someone was, the pastor will sing their praises at the funeral. Why? This spares the feelings of those who are left behind.

The truth is that not everyone who dies led a good life and no one automatically goes to heaven. We are given one life to live and after that judgment awaits us. God punishes sin, but is merciful to everyone who humbles themselves before Him.

The wages of sin is death, but the gift of God is
eternal life in Christ Jesus our Lord.
Romans 6:23

His mercy extends to those who fear Him,
from generation to generation.
Luke 1:50

NO SLAP ON THE WRIST

God is the judge who judges a person's life and then determines the appropriate punishment. God's judgment is not a light slap on the wrist. We will all be called to give account for our actions. If it looks like the godless have the upper hand and that God is powerless, think again.

God does not call sinners to account immediately, but gives them a chance to repent. God's grace is not weakness; it is a last appeal to sinners to come to salvation.

Do you show contempt for the riches of His kindness, forbearance and patience, not realizing that God's kindness is intended to lead you to repentance?
Romans 2:4

The Lord our God is merciful and forgiving, even though we have rebelled against Him.
Daniel 9:9

LOSING YOUR LIFE FOR JESUS

Everything revolves around Jesus. There is no reconcil-iation with the Father, no new life or forgiveness of sins without Him. To reject Jesus and deny His authority, position and status is to incur God's wrath. The mes-sage is clear – reject and deny Jesus or deny yourself. Pray that Jesus will remain your all, even though you lose your life, because without Jesus we have nothing.

Anyone who rejected the law of Moses died without mercy on the testimony of two or three witnesses. How much more severely do you think someone deserves to be punished who has trampled the Son of God underfoot, who has treated as an unholy thing the blood of the covenant that sanctified them, and who has insulted the Spirit of grace?
Hebrews 10:28-29

"No one who denies the Son has the Father; whoever acknowledges the Son has the Father also."
1 John 2:23

JESUS PAID THE PRICE IN FULL

No one can take Jesus' life – He freely gives it. This is what makes the crucifixion so remarkable. Jesus willingly suffered for us. For three hours Jesus hung on the cross and was forsaken by God; the curse of sin and the devil upon Him. With His cry, "It is finished!" the price was paid. Lord Jesus, our Master!

"The reason My Father loves Me is that I lay down My life – only to take it up again. No one takes it from Me, but I lay it down of My own accord. I have authority to lay it down and authority to take it up again. This command I received from My Father."

John 10:17-18

Jesus called out with a loud voice, "Father, into Your hands I commit My spirit." When He had said this, He breathed His last.

Luke 23:46

SET FREE!

To be set free from sin is a wonderful reality that every disciple of Jesus can experience. We all know the burden and strain that sin places on our lives and then to have the shackles of sin broken is such a powerful testimony of the reality of Jesus in our lives.

Once we are free, we must guard this freedom and not dabble with past sins again. Guard your salvation with zeal and determination. Jesus will set you free if you truly desire to be free.

It is for freedom that Christ has set us free.
Stand firm, then, and do not let yourselves be
burdened again by a yoke of slavery.
Galatians 5:1

"If the Son sets you free, you will be free indeed."
John 8:36

GOD SAVES US

Sin not only makes us want to hide from God, but also alienates us from Him because it places us in opposition to Him. This is why Jesus came to earth, so that He could bear the punishment for our sins on the cross. Through His death and resurrection we can be united with God in eternal life and never have to be afraid of Him again. Jesus' death put an end to the judgment of those who accept His offer of salvation. We never need to hide from God because He saves us.

Therefore, brothers and sisters, since we have confidence to enter the Most Holy Place by the blood of Jesus by a new and living way opened for us through the curtain, that is, His body, and since we have a great priest over the house of God, let us draw near to God with a sincere heart and with the full assurance that faith brings, having our hearts sprinkled to cleanse us from a guilty conscience and having our bodies washed with pure water.
Hebrews 10:19-22

Therefore, there is now no condemnation for those who are in Christ Jesus.
Romans 8:1

THE FINAL REDEMPTION

God not only grants us life in the midst of death in this world, but also promises eternal freedom from all suffering, sin and death. God also promises that creation will be freed from the effects of sin. In the midst of this promise and ministry is Jesus Christ – central and perfect. No promise is fulfilled outside of Him and there is no life outside of Him. Jesus is the one who redeems us from our sinful nature and our past.

The creation was subjected to frustration, not by its own choice, but by the will of the one who subjected it, in hope that the creation itself will be liberated from its bondage to decay and brought into the freedom and glory of the children of God.

Romans 8:20-21

Israel, put your hope in the LORD, for with the LORD is unfailing love and with Him is full redemption.

Psalm 130:7

PERFECT AND COMPLETE

We will finally be made whole when we stand before God and made perfect and complete in every aspect of our lives. This will happen in one of two ways: The first is the second coming of Jesus, which is the final declaration about sin and suffering. The other way is when we die. If we die in Christ we will see God face to face and become perfect in spirit, soul and body. Everyone who dies in Christ already has this life.

"He will wipe every tear from their eyes. There will be no more death" or mourning or crying or pain, for the old order of things has passed away.
Revelation 21:4

Now it is God who makes both us and you stand firm in Christ.
2 Corinthians 1:21

A PROMISED SAVIOR

God knew beforehand about all the sorrow and grief that would be in the world and He offered Jesus as the solution, reconciliation, healing and restoration. God is the answer to everything. Man's sin does not take God by surprise. He is always in control, even when we lose control. We have limited perspective and insight, but He knows everything. When Adam and Eve sinned, God said that He would send a Savior who would crush Satan underfoot as they had not been able to do.

"I will put enmity between you and the woman, and between your offspring and hers; He will crush your head, and you will strike His heel."
Genesis 3:15

You know that it was not with perishable things such as silver or gold that you were redeemed from the empty way of life handed down to you from your ancestors, but with the precious blood of Christ, a lamb without blemish or defect.
1 Peter 1:18-19

IF WE WANT TO BE FREE

Jesus will set us free if we truly want to find freedom. But sometimes we don't want to let go of the sins in our lives. We pray for freedom from sin, but when the temptation arises we give in to it. Our inner rebellion against God is our greatest enemy. Confess your rebellion and see how sin loses its power over you.

> Then I acknowledged my sin to You and did not cover up my iniquity. I said, "I will confess my transgressions to the LORD." And You forgave the guilt of my sin. Therefore let all the faithful pray to You while You may be found.
>
> Psalm 32:5-6

> If you declare with your mouth, "Jesus is Lord," and believe in your heart that God raised Him from the dead, you will be saved.
>
> Romans 10:9

AN ONGOING PROCESS

Can we be freed from sin and live sinless lives? Yes, we can be saved from our sins, but no, we can't lead sinless lives. The more we come to know Jesus, the more we recognize those things in our lives that are not in line with Jesus' character.

Our lives on earth are a continual confrontation with sin until the Lord Jesus returns. Our path of purity and holiness is an ongoing one in which we experience Jesus.

If we walk in the light, as He is in the light, we have fellowship with one another, and the blood of Jesus, His Son, purifies us from all sin.
1 John 1:7

Jesus said, "Truly I tell you, people can be forgiven all their sins and every slander they utter."
Mark 3:28

NOTHING BUT THE BLOOD OF JESUS

The blood of Christ purifies us from all sin. This means that there is no sin known to man from which Jesus cannot free us. To confess and repent is the way to salvation. We don't have to be kept prisoner by any sin because Jesus is willing and able to set us free.

You also were included in Christ when you heard the message of truth, the gospel of your salvation. When you believed, you were marked in Him with a seal, the promised Holy Spirit, who is a deposit guaranteeing our inheritance until the redemption of those who are God's possession – to the praise of His glory.
Ephesians 1:13-14

You will again have compassion on us;
You will tread our sins underfoot and hurl
all our iniquities into the depths of the sea.
Micah 7:19

JESUS, SAVIOR OF ALL MANKIND

Jesus is the Savior of all people, but especially of those who believe. However, God is gracious to people all over the world, irrespective of who they are or what they believe. It doesn't matter whether they are Baptists or Buddhists. It doesn't matter if people aggressively resist God or are simply ignorant of His existence. His grace shines on them every day and all can come to Him for salvation, regardless.

That is why we labor and strive, because we have put our hope in the living God, who is the Savior of all people, and especially of those who believe.
1 Timothy 4:10

"He causes His sun to rise on the evil and the good, and sends rain on the righteous and the unrighteous."
Matthew 5:45

THE MOST LIBERATED PEOPLE ON EARTH

God is the Savior of those who believe, to those who have entrusted their soul to Jesus to give them everlasting life. They might not be freed from circumstances, but they are still the most liberated people on earth because they have been freed from Satan's hold.

Now the Lord is the Spirit, and where the
Spirit of the Lord is, there is freedom.
2 Corinthians 3:17

Thanks be to God that, though you used to be
slaves to sin, you have come to obey from your
heart the pattern of teaching that has now claimed
your allegiance. You have been set free from sin
and have become slaves to righteousness.
Romans 6:17-18

GOD'S PEOPLE

People who believe in Jesus as the Lord and Savior of their souls get back up after they have been knocked down because God saves them in an extraordinary way. Their fight for the preservation of their lives turns into a joy because no one and nothing can take true life away from them. The Bible says of such people that "the world was not worthy of them" (Hebrews 11:38). These are God's people.

In Christ Jesus you are all children of God through faith, for all of you who were baptized into Christ have clothed yourselves with Christ.
Galatians 3:26-27

Yet to all who did receive Him, to those who believed in His name, He gave the right to become children of God – children born not of natural descent, nor of human decision or a husband's will, but born of God.
John 1:12-13

THE DIVIDENDS OF SIN

Hard and unrepentant hearts must be called to account. God's judgment is fair and He will pay dividends to everyone who opposes Him. This isn't the kind of treasure we want to accumulate at the end of our lives. Sin holds no blessing for us. The only good thing about sin is that God sets us free from it. We don't have to live with sin or receive God's judgment because of it.

Because of your stubbornness and your unrepentant heart, you are storing up wrath against yourself for the day of God's wrath, when His righteous judgment will be revealed.

Romans 2:5

"But I tell you that everyone will have to give account on the day of judgment for every empty word they have spoken. For by your words you will be acquitted, and by your words you will be condemned."

Matthew 12:36-37

DON'T ARGUE WITH NON-BELIEVERS

In every generation you get "intellectuals" who write off any faith in God as unlearned, superstitious and even backward. Don't try to argue with people like this. Salvation is not intellectual, but divine. Don't concern yourself with such arguments, but allow God to be the Ruler in your life with all your heart and mind.

Guard what has been entrusted to your care. Turn away from godless chatter and the opposing ideas of what is falsely called knowledge, which some have professed and in so doing have departed from the faith.
1 Timothy 6:20-21

Keep reminding God's people of these things. Warn them before God against quarreling about words; it is of no value, and only ruins those who listen.
2 Timothy 2:14

THE CURSE HAS BEEN BROKEN

The curse of sin is precisely that – a curse. Sin might be pleasant for a moment, but it brings an incalculable burden on those who partake in it. The cost is so great that Jesus had to die to pay it. Through Jesus we receive deliverance from sin and its curse. Jesus paid the price for us.

When He was hung on the cross, He took
upon Himself the curse for our wrongdoing.
For it is written in the Scriptures, "Cursed
is everyone who is hung on a tree."
Galatians 3:13 NLT

In Him we have redemption through His blood,
the forgiveness of sins, in accordance with
the riches of God's grace.
Ephesians 1:7

FREEDOM IN CHRIST

Jesus is the only one who can deliver us from sin and set us free. Only through Jesus and the redemption He brings can we set out on the path that God originally planned for us. Once you have been set free, don't become bound by sin in your life again.

It is for freedom that Christ has set us free. Stand firm, then, and do not let yourselves be burdened again by a yoke of slavery.

Galatians 5:1

Grace and peace to you from Him who is, and who was, and who is to come … and from Jesus Christ, who is the faithful witness, the firstborn from the dead, and the ruler of the kings of the earth. To Him who loves us and has freed us from our sins by His blood, and has made us to be a kingdom and priests to serve His God and Father – to Him be glory and power for ever and ever! Amen.

Revelation 1:4-6

JESUS ALONE REDEEMS US

Laws and corrective action can't free people from sin. Only Jesus can restore our fall from grace and redeem us. We are free to win others for Christ, but no longer control others to get what we want. We regard them as worthy and treat them with love and respect.

As believers we can stand in unity, as God created us to be. This is all possible through the redemption and salvation we receive in Christ.

Therefore, since we have been justified through faith, we have peace with God through our Lord Jesus Christ, through whom we have gained access by faith into this grace in which we now stand. And we boast in the hope of the glory of God.
Romans 5:1-2

All are justified freely by His grace through the redemption that came by Christ Jesus.
Romans 3:24

SELF-JUSTIFICATION DOESN'T WORK

Justification is the process whereby someone is declared righteous, innocent from crime and free from punishment. Self-justification means that I do this myself. To try to justify ourselves means that we don't allow God to do it. We can't justify ourselves and neither can other people – only Jesus can justify us, making us righteous and setting us free.

He said to them, "You are the ones who justify yourselves in the eyes of others, but God knows your hearts. What people value highly is detestable in God's sight."
Luke 16:15

"I know your deeds, that you are neither cold nor hot. I wish you were either one or the other! So, because you are lukewarm – neither hot nor cold – I am about to spit you out of My mouth."
Revelation 3:15-16

A SPECK OF SAWDUST

There are too many advice-givers today who themselves need guidance – too many who want to tell others how to live, but don't apply their advice to their own lives. The only ones who are justified to talk about the sawdust in others' eyes are the ones who are open and honest about their own speck of sawdust. The only One who doesn't have even the smallest speck of sawdust is Jesus and this makes Him the best Guide and Advisor. Don't try to hide or justify the speck in your own eye; ask Jesus to remove it for you. He is the only One who can help you.

"Why do you look at the speck of sawdust in your brother's eye and pay no attention to the plank in your own eye? How can you say to your brother, 'Let me take the speck out of your eye,' when all the time there is a plank in your own eye? You hypocrite, first take the plank out of your own eye, and then you will see clearly to remove the speck from your brother's eye."

Matthew 7:3-5

FORGIVENESS FOR BETRAYAL

How could Judas betray Jesus for a month's salary after everything he had seen and heard? Perhaps Judas became disappointed in Jesus. What do you expect from Him? Healing, prosperity, a job promotion? How would you react if Jesus disappointed you? There is salvation and forgiveness for everyone – even betrayers. The Lord Jesus forgives and cleanses us completely – even when we have betrayed Him – and gives us a new life in His name.

Then Satan entered Judas, called Iscariot, one of the Twelve. And Judas went to the chief priests and the officers of the temple guard and discussed with them how he might betray Jesus. They were delighted and agreed to give him money.

Luke 22:3-5

"Come now, let us settle the matter," says the Lord. "Though your sins are like scarlet, they shall be as white as snow; though they are red as crimson, they shall be like wool."

Isaiah 1:18

UNCONDITIONAL FORGIVENESS

Unconditional love is demonstrated in forgiveness. There are no conditions to forgiveness, just as there are no conditions to love. When we are confronted by Christ's love for us on the cross, all our rebellion and stubbornness is brought to the fore. Love and forgiveness have the ability to reach into the depths of a person's heart and bring everything that hides there out into the open.

Then Peter came to Jesus and asked, "Lord, how many times shall I forgive my brother or sister who sins against me? Up to seven times?" Jesus answered, "I tell you, not seven times, but seventy-seven times."

Matthew 18:21-22

Blessed is the one whose transgressions are forgiven, whose sins are covered. Blessed is the one whose sin the Lord does not count against them and in whose spirit is no deceit.

Psalm 32:1-2

NO PAYMENT PLAN

Sometimes it seems that people think that God's services and love are on loan. They believe they must do good deeds as a form of payment. They miss the boat completely! There isn't a payment plan because Jesus has paid for everything in full. God doesn't do good things to buy our affection, He does it because He is good. He continually invites us to be in a fellowship with Him. God is not on loan, but is freely available to anyone who comes to Him.

On the last and greatest day of the festival, Jesus stood and said in a loud voice, "Let anyone who is thirsty come to Me and drink."
John 7:37

"Very truly I tell you, whoever hears My word and believes Him who sent Me has eternal life and will not be judged but has crossed over from death to life."
John 5:24

GOD FORGIVES AND PURIFIES

Forgiveness is purification and purification is forgiveness. God doesn't give the one without the other. God forgives and cleanses a sinner; it is as if they have never sinned. God forgives and forgets and doesn't think about those sins again. Trust God to forgive your sins and to cleanse you. He will heal you.

If we say that we have no sin, we deceive ourselves, and the truth is not in us. If we confess our sins, He is faithful and just to forgive us our sins and to cleanse us from all unrighteousness.
1 John 1:8-9 NKJV

As far as the east is from the west, so far has He removed our transgressions from us. As a father has compassion on his children, so the LORD has compassion on those who fear Him.
Psalm 103:12-13

THE GOOD NEWS!

The sins we have committed against God can never be repaid. Sin destroys our lives, but when we bow before God He removes the guilt of our transgressions. This is why the gospel message is such good news! God's forgiveness does not come easy, however. It comes at the high cost of Christ's blood.

"The servant fell on his knees before him. 'Be patient with me,' he begged, 'and I will pay back everything.' The servant's master took pity on him, canceled the debt and let him go."

Matthew 18:26-27

He was pierced for our transgressions, He was crushed for our iniquities; the punishment that brought us peace was on Him, and by His wounds we are healed.

Isaiah 53:5

CLEANSED BY THE BLOOD OF JESUS

God's forgiveness leaves us speechless. He moved mountains to restore our relationship with Him – His forgiveness is complete and in full. He sent His Son Jesus to set us free from all sin. There need not be the least stain of sin in our lives, because Jesus' blood removed it all.

God presented Jesus as the sacrifice for sin. People are made right with God when they believe that Jesus sacrificed His life, shedding his blood. This sacrifice shows that God was being fair when He held back and did not punish those who sinned in times past, for He was looking ahead and including them in what He would do in this present time. God did this to demonstrate His righteousness, for He Himself is fair and just, and He declares sinners to be right in His sight when they believe in Jesus.

Romans 3:25-26 NLT

He was delivered over to death for our sins and was raised to life for our justification.

Romans 4:25

AUGUST

FOLLOWING THE LIGHT

When Jesus spoke again to the people, He said, "I am the light of the world. Whoever follows Me will never walk in darkness, but will have the light of life." John 8:12

THE LIGHT CALLS US TO HIM

God didn't create man to inhabit the earth and busy ourselves with all sorts of things; He created us to be in a relationship with His Son. God is a God of relationships. He is concerned with giving and receiving love. All God's blessings lie hidden in a relationship with Him through Jesus Christ. A relationship with Jesus is our most important calling.

His divine power has given us everything we need for a godly life through our knowledge of Him who called us by His own glory and goodness.
2 Peter 1:3

If I have the gift of prophecy and can fathom all mysteries and all knowledge, and if I have a faith that can move mountains, but do not have love, I am nothing. If I give all I possess to the poor and give over my body to hardship that I may boast, but do not have love, I gain nothing.
1 Corinthians 13:2-3

JESUS IS THE KEY

God wants to be in a relationship with you through His Son. If this is not also your heart's desire then you are at odds with God's plan for you. You might want God to focus on your well-being and happiness, while God wants you to focus on His Son. Now is the time for a breakthrough. Forget what is behind and reach out to what lies ahead: Jesus Christ, the joy of God. Jesus is the key to your future.

Jesus replied: "'Love the LORD your God with all your heart and with all your soul and with all your mind.' This is the first and greatest commandment."
Matthew 22:37-38

We do this by keeping our eyes on Jesus, the champion who initiates and perfects our faith. Because of the joy awaiting Him, He endured the cross, disregarding its shame. Now He is seated in the place of honor beside God's throne.
Hebrews 12:2 NLT

OUR PRIMARY PURPOSE ON EARTH

There are many people who never realize their true purpose. Even though they might be very successful in life, they remain empty inside. This is because they never experience the deepest fulfilment in life – a relationship with Jesus Christ. This is our primary purpose on earth. Total fulfilment in life can only lie in a relationship with God.

Yet for us there is but one God, the Father, from whom all things came and for whom we live; and there is but one Lord, Jesus Christ, through whom all things came and through whom we live.

1 Corinthians 8:6

We know that we have come to know Him if we keep His commands. Whoever says, "I know Him," but does not do what He commands is a liar, and the truth is not in that person. But if anyone obeys His word, love for God is truly made complete in them.

1 John 2:3-5

OUR GREATEST FULFILMENT IN LIFE

Many people think that going to church is enough, but it doesn't guarantee a relationship with the Father. Why does it take us years before we obediently kneel before Jesus in our chosen calling? Turn to Jesus and ask Him to be our Lord, our Friend and our life's greatest fulfilment.

You will show me the way of life, granting me the joy of Your presence and the pleasures of living with You forever.
Psalm 16:11 NLT

The LORD will guide you always; He will satisfy your needs in a sun-scorched land and will strengthen your frame. You will be like a well-watered garden, like a spring whose waters never fail.
Isaiah 58:11

PEACEMAKERS ARE CHILDREN OF GOD

The peacemakers Jesus speaks of in Matthew 5:9 iden-
tify themselves directly with the family of God – they
are children of the Lord.

Children of God take after their Father: Their
character and lives are of such a nature that they serve
people with peace. They speak gracious words to others. As Jesus says, do this "that you may be children of
your Father in heaven" (Matthew 5:45).

*Let us pursue the things which make for peace and the
things by which one may edify another.*
Romans 14:19 NKJV

*Blessed are the peacemakers, for they will
be called children of God.*
Matthew 5:9

*Let the peace of Christ rule in your
hearts, since as members of one body
you were called to peace.*
Colossians 3:15

JESUS RESTORES OUR RELATIONSHIPS

Jesus not only came to restore our relationship with God, but also to break down the dividing walls between us and others so that we may love each other as we love ourselves. Jesus didn't come to earth to make us religious, to set up denominations or to single out certain people above others.

God is a god of relationship and His ministry is a healing balm for our lives, relationships and all of humanity.

Love prospers when a fault is forgiven, but dwelling on it separates close friends.

Proverbs 17:9 NLT

"If your brother or sister sins, go and point out their fault, just between the two of you. If they listen to you, you have won them over."

Matthew 18:15

LIGHT IS ESSENTIAL

Light is the symbol of truth, goodness and enlighten-ment. We all have a "light" by which we live. We de-termine the course of our lives by it. Jesus warns that we must watch out because if the light in our lives is darkness, we are in trouble. We must ask ourselves, "How much of the light in us is darkness?" We need a revelation of the light in order to be discerning. This is why a relationship with Jesus is not just an option – it is essential.

> "See to it, then, that the light within you is not darkness. Therefore, if your whole body is full of light, and no part of it dark, it will be just as full of light as when a lamp shines its light on you."
>
> Luke 11:35-36

> "You are the light of the world. A town built on a hill cannot be hidden. Neither do people light a lamp and put it under a bowl. Instead they put it on its stand, and it gives light to everyone in the house. In the same way, let your light shine before others, that they may see your good deeds and glorify your Father in heaven."
>
> Matthew 5:14-16

WHY DID JESUS COME TO EARTH?

There are many ways to answer this question, one of which is to say that Jesus came to restore relationships. Jesus came to die for our sins and to rise from the dead in order to give us new life. Why? Because from birth we are enemies of God and are far from Him.

Jesus came to restore our relationship with God so that we could love Him with all our heart, all our soul, and all our strength.

"For even the Son of Man did not come to be served, but to serve, and to give His life as a ransom for many."
Mark 10:45

All this is from God, who reconciled us to Himself through Christ and gave us the ministry of reconciliation: that God was reconciling the world to Himself in Christ, not counting people's sins against them.
2 Corinthians 5:18-19

DO WE HAVE ACCESS TO GOD?

Jesus is near the Father and has direct access to Him. There is no break in the relationship or the slightest estrangement. We, however, are not able to have this same kind of relationship because of the sin that separates us from God.

Only Jesus is able to bridge the gap between us and God. He invites us to be reconciled with God. Ask Jesus to reconcile you with God today, and you will have access to the Father.

No one has ever seen God, but the one and only Son, who is Himself God and is in closest relationship with the Father, has made Him known.

John 1:18

For God was in Christ, reconciling the world to Himself, no longer counting people's sins against them. And He gave us this wonderful message of reconciliation.

2 Corinthians 5:19 NLT

THE BLESSING AND CURSE OF EMOTIONS

There are times when you might feel that God is far away, that you aren't good enough for Him, that He doesn't hear you, that you are struggling to survive on your own, that you are a disappointment or that you are suffering and God isn't helping you. Emotions can be a blessing, but also a curse because they can lead us away from God's truth.

We tend to place our emotions above God's Word. We sometimes feel far removed from God because that is what our emotions dictate. The wonderful thing is that our emotions will remain in tune with Jesus when we remain faithful to Him.

All the ways of the LORD are loving and faithful
toward those who keep the demands of His covenant.
Psalm 25:10

May integrity and uprightness protect me,
because my hope, LORD, is in You.
Psalm 25:21

POWER AND STATUS

We mustn't compete with each other for power and control. The one who serves is leader over the others. This is a powerful lesson that Jesus teaches us. God isn't concerned with position or status, but with relationships.

If your position and status give you a sense of worth, then it might be that you have broken relationships in your life. Take a closer look at your relationship with God.

> *Jesus said, "The last will be first,*
> *and the first will be last."*
> Matthew 20:16

> *"Everyone who has left houses or brothers or*
> *father or mother or wife or children or fields for*
> *My sake will receive a hundred times as much*
> *and will inherit eternal life. Many who are first*
> *will be last, and many who are last will be first."*
> Matthew 19:29-30

ALL ARE EQUAL

There is no rank among God's children, only relationships. Seniority isn't established by power and authority, but by obedience and love.

Our relationship with God confirms our identity and worth, and when this relationship is absent, we seek a position and rank to fulfil it. In a relationship with God, everyone is equal and God's character enfolds everyone, whether young, old or weak.

There is neither Jew nor Gentile, neither
slave nor free, nor is there male and female,
for you are all one in Christ Jesus.
Galatians 3:28

"Whoever wants to become great among you
must be your servant, and whoever wants to be
first must be slave of all."
Mark 10:44

UNITY WITH THE SON

Through Jesus Christ we have access to wonderful things. We can call God Father – previously unthinkable. We become partners in His nature – previously impossible. We become members of His family – previously children of wrath. We share in God's unity with the Son. Jesus Christ doesn't make us religious – He does far more than that. In Jesus and through Jesus, God gives us the ability to know Him, to be part of His life and to experience that life on earth.

Consequently, you are no longer foreigners and strangers, but fellow citizens with God's people and also members of His household.
Ephesians 2:19

We know also that the Son of God has come and has given us understanding, so that we may know Him who is true. And we are in Him who is true by being in His Son Jesus Christ. He is the true God and eternal life.
1 John 5:20

ATTITUDE IS IMPORTANT

Some people think that unity means having the same opinion as others. If this were true unity would never be possible! Unity has more to do with attitudes and less to do with opinions. It is the attitude of the heart. When people stand in humility and dependence before God there is unity. Unity has to do with having the same love – having the same attitude as Jesus. There can only be harmony if we have the same attitude as Jesus.

"My prayer is not for them alone. I pray also for those who will believe in Me through their message, that all of them may be one, Father, just as You are in Me and I am in You. May they also be in Us so that the world may believe that You have sent Me."

John 17:20-21

"Holy Father, protect them by the power of Your name so that they will be united just as We are."

John 17:11 NLT

THERE IS NO BLESSING IN DISUNITY

There can be no unity where believers live in unrest and disobedience to Jesus, outside of the character of their Master. Where there is disunity, people live outside of the truth of Christ. We pray for blessing and prosperity, but God says it is in Jesus. It doesn't help to pray if we are disobedient. It's time to start praying for the right thing – for forgiveness. God has opened the way to blessings – walk in it.

*Make my joy complete by being
like-minded, having the same love, being one
in spirit and of one mind.*
Philippians 2:2

*How good and pleasant it is when God's people
live together in unity! It is as if the dew of Hermon
were falling on Mount Zion. For there the LORD
bestows His blessing, even life forevermore.*
Psalm 133:1, 3

AN ATTITUDE OF HUMILITY

As believers we are able to live out the same attitude as Christ. Jesus lowered Himself from His position with God to reach us. He then lowered Himself even further by laying down His life for us. This is an attitude of unity. Those who have received Christ are free to join the ranks of the humble and simple. They are wise and their identity lies in Jesus. Goodness and favor follows them even though they do not look for it. These are God's people.

Live in harmony with one another. Do not be proud, but be willing to associate with people of low position. Do not be conceited.
Romans 12:16

"... I in them and You in Me – so that they may be brought to complete unity. Then the world will know that You sent Me and have loved them even as You have loved Me."
John 17:23

URGED TO KEEP THE UNITY OF THE SPIRIT

The Scriptures below reveal an earnest call for unity and love. Believers are called to have a relationship with Jesus and with others around them. To live out this calling in a worthy way is a serious business. We are urged to "make every effort to keep the unity of the Spirit." There is no doubt as to how important this is to God.

As a prisoner for the Lord, then, I urge you to live a life worthy of the calling you have received. Be completely humble and gentle; be patient, bearing with one another in love. Make every effort to keep the unity of the Spirit through the bond of peace.

Ephesians 4:1-3

May the God who gives endurance and encouragement give you the same attitude of mind toward each other that Christ Jesus had.

Romans 15:5

GOD'S PEOPLE ARE EXALTED

Those who are exalted by God don't need to fight to achieve it or to keep it. God grants it and takes it away as He sees fit. These people are in keeping with God's will and enjoy peace in their lives as a result.

Our greatest profit is Christ and He will exalt us at the right time. People who are agreeable to God are free people, whole people, life-giving and set apart.

"What good is it for someone to gain the whole world, yet forfeit their soul? Or what can anyone give in exchange for their soul?"
Mark 8:36-37

Humble yourselves before the Lord, and He will lift you up.
James 4:10

FOREIGNERS AND STRANGERS

We are either "foreigners and strangers" to the world, or to God. It's either one or the other. The invitation to God's children is to stand unashamedly "outside the camp" because we don't belong in the world's camps. We belong to one another and we are not of this world.

Let us, then, go to Him outside the camp,
bearing the disgrace He bore. For here we do
not have an enduring city, but we are
looking for the city that is to come.
Hebrews 13:13-14

Dear friends, I urge you, as foreigners and
exiles, to abstain from sinful desires, which
wage war against your soul.
1 Peter 2:11

"If you belonged to the world, it would love
you as its own. As it is, you do not belong
to the world, but I have chosen
you out of the world."
John 15:19

THE FATHER'S HOUSE

God has a household that He loving and carefully keeps and as God's children we are expected to do the same. If we fail in this area we have betrayed our faith in Jesus. Faith in Christ is very practical. To look after your family means to meet their needs. It is your duty to protect them and to ask God for wisdom and guidance.

Fear the LORD and serve Him with all faithfulness ... But if serving the LORD seems undesirable to you, then choose for yourselves this day whom you will serve ... But as for me and my household, we will serve the LORD.
Joshua 24:14-15

Whoever brings ruin on their family will inherit only wind, and the fool will be servant to the wise.
Proverbs 11:29

CARE FOR YOUR FAMILY

It is wrong to neglect your family for the sake of religion. Even if they turn against you because you have chosen Jesus, you must still care for them to the best of your ability and remain dedicated to them. This is the character of God and how the Spirit of God works. True faith in Jesus joins people together in love, protection and care.

Anyone who does not provide for their relatives, and especially for their own household, has denied the faith and is worse than an unbeliever.

1 Timothy 5:8

Do not repay anyone evil for evil. Be careful to do what is right in the eyes of everyone. If it is possible, as far as it depends on you, live at peace with everyone.

Romans 12:17-18

DO YOU NEED A HEART DOCTOR?

No one is invisible to God. We can't hide anything from God, especially what is in the hidden depths of our hearts. God cares about our hearts and is the only one who can judge what is in it. Is your heart submissive to God or have you hardened your heart? Don't rebel against God; ask Him to remove your heart of stone and to give you a heart of flesh once more.

Nothing in all creation is hidden from God's sight. Everything is uncovered and laid bare before the eyes of Him to whom we must give account.

Hebrews 4:13

I will give you a new heart and put a new spirit in you; I will remove from you your heart of stone and give you a heart of flesh.

Ezekiel 36:26

LIKE A CHILD

We place importance in status and power, but God focuses on the children, the weak and the defenseless. Born-again believers are called children of God and are taught to have faith like a child. Take off your mask before God and allow Him to restore your childlike faith. Your whole life will change as your faith grows.

Jesus said, "Let the little children come to Me, and do not hinder them, for the kingdom of heaven belongs to such as these."
Matthew 19:14

And He said: "Truly I tell you, unless you change and become like little children, you will never enter the kingdom of heaven. Therefore, whoever takes the lowly position of this child is the greatest in the kingdom of heaven."
Matthew 18:2-4

TRUE POWER

Power is not demonstrated by muscles and a display of strength, but in the simplicity of God. God's greatest show of power was in the form of a lamb – the Lamb of God. God is the way and He leads to true life. Walk in this way with childlike faith and simplicity.

The Spirit you received does not make you slaves,
so that you live in fear again; rather, the Spirit you
received brought about your adoption to sonship.
And by Him we cry, "Abba, Father."
Romans 8:15

Follow God's example, therefore,
as dearly loved children and walk in the way
of love, just as Christ loved us and gave Himself
up for us as a fragrant offering and sacrifice to God.
Ephesians 5:1-2

THE CROWN OF GOD'S CREATION

God loves you and accepts you – with the full knowledge of all your failures. You don't have to meet certain standards to qualify for God's acceptance and love. He declares your worth regardless of your accomplishments or image. You are the most valuable being in the universe, not because you are cute or good, but because you are the crown of God's creation.

*For we are God's handiwork, created
in Christ Jesus to do good works, which
God prepared in advance for us to do.*
Ephesians 2:10

*What is mankind that You are mindful of them,
human beings that You care for them? You have
made them a little lower than the angels and
crowned them with glory and honor. You made
them rulers over the works of Your hands;
You put everything under their feet.*
Psalm 8:4-6

AN OPEN INVITATION

God invites you to accept Him for who He is. He has already accepted you, but you have the final say. You have to decide whether you will accept Him and become part of His family. The choice is yours.

> *"Here I am! I stand at the door and knock.*
> *If anyone hears My voice and opens the door,*
> *I will come in and eat with that*
> *person, and they with Me."*
> *Revelation 3:20*

> *"You will seek Me and find Me when you seek*
> *Me with all your heart. I will be found*
> *by you," declares the LORD.*
> *Jeremiah 29:13-14*

A CHOICE WITH ETERNAL CONSEQUENCES

The greatest tragedy is when people see God's invitation and do not accept it. He stands and knocks, but only we can open the door and invite Him in. This is the greatest decision we can make in life – one with eternal consequences.

> The LORD said to Samuel, "Do not consider
> his appearance or his height, for I have rejected him.
> The LORD does not look at the things people look at.
> People look at the outward appearance, but the
> LORD looks at the heart."
>
> 1 Samuel 16:7

> Yet to all who did receive Him, to those
> who believed in His name, He gave the
> right to become children of God.
>
> John 1:12

ACCEPTANCE BY WHOM?

The desire for acceptance is a very strong force in our lives. For this reason it is also very dangerous. When disobedience to God brings us acceptance by others, we need to watch out. Like Jesus, accept rejection from people and acceptance by God and you will see that you receive more than you will ever need.

Submit yourselves, then, to God. Resist the devil, and he will flee from you. Come near to God and He will come near to you. Wash your hands, you sinners, and purify your hearts, you double-minded.

James 4:7-8

"If the world hates you, keep in mind that it hated Me first. If you belonged to the world, it would love you as its own. As it is, you do not belong to the world, but I have chosen you out of the world. That is why the world hates you."

John 15:18-19

A LACK OF LOVE FOR GOD

A lack of love towards Jesus' disciples is a direct lack of love for God. We might try not to talk negatively of Jesus, but we don't mind gossiping about and bad-mouthing His disciples. We don't realize that our fighting, cheating and bitterness is unacceptable to God. Are you acting in a loveless way towards fellow disciples? If so, you are demonstrating a lack of love for God.

"We all fell to the ground, and I heard a voice saying to me in Aramaic, 'Saul, Saul, why do you persecute Me? It is hard for you to kick against the goads.'"
Acts 26:14

Accept one another, then, just as Christ accepted you, in order to bring praise to God.
Romans 15:7

NO AIRS AND GRACES

If we are anxious to please God then we need to drop our masks and airs and graces. Don't try to be clever, but stand before God in all simplicity. This is how Jesus is. It pleases God when we serve those who are less privileged than ourselves and associate with them.

He has shown you, O mortal, what is good.
And what does the LORD require of you?
To act justly and to love mercy and to walk
humbly with your God.
Micah 6:8

Who is wise and understanding among you?
Let them show it by their good life, by deeds done
in the humility that comes from wisdom.
James 3:13

All of you, be like-minded, be sympathetic,
love one another, be compassionate and humble.
1 Peter 3:8

SIMPLICITY IS SIMPLY GREAT

We don't think much of the simple, ordinary things. We all want to be set apart as exceptional people. But in Matthew 11:25 (NLT), Jesus says, "O Father, Lord of heaven and earth, thank You for hiding these things from those who think themselves wise and clever, and for revealing them to the childlike."

Humble yourselves, therefore, under God's
mighty hand, that He may lift you up in due time.
1 Peter 5:6

He sets on high those who are lowly,
and those who mourn are lifted to safety.
Job 5:11

Better to be of a humble spirit with the lowly,
than to divide the spoil with the proud.
Proverbs 16:19 NKJV

SEPTEMBER

LET YOUR LIGHT SHINE

*"In the same way, let your light shine before others,
that they may see your good deeds and glorify
your Father in heaven." Matthew 5:16*

OBEDIENCE AND SUBMISSION

Obedience and submission go together hand in hand. A submissive heart does not consider itself better than others. Obedience means to do what you are told. If you want to be in God's favor, ask Him to teach you how to be submissive and obedient. Then you will shine as a light to the world – just like Jesus.

As obedient children, do not conform to the evil desires you had when you lived in ignorance. But just as He who called you is holy, so be holy in all you do.
1 Peter 1:14-15

Peter and the other apostles replied: "We must obey God rather than human beings!"
Acts 5:29

Submit yourselves, then, to God. Resist the devil, and he will flee from you.
James 4:7

THE PERFECT EXAMPLE

Jesus never considered Himself better than others, even though He was God. Jesus knew how to stand perfectly under God's authority in His relationships with other people.

Many people desire God's favor and even pray for it, but are not willing to submit to Him and be obedient. Their prayers will never be answered. We need to follow Jesus' example and be submissive and obedient.

> *"If you are willing and obedient, you will eat*
> *the good things of the land; but if you resist*
> *and rebel, you will be devoured by the sword."*
> *Isaiah 1:19-20*

> *In your relationships with one another,*
> *have the same mindset as Christ Jesus.*
> *Philippians 2:5*

THE BEST PLACE TO BE

God's character is reflected in submission and obedience. We live in a world where submission means to be oppressed and obedience means to have no freedom. However, submission has nothing to do with oppression and everything to do with dependence on God. Stay dependent on Him – it's the best place to be.

Keep me from deceitful ways; be gracious to me and teach me Your law. I have chosen the way of faithfulness; I have set my heart on Your laws. I hold fast to Your statutes, Lord.
Psalm 119:29-31

Submit to one another out of reverence for Christ.
Ephesians 5:21

SUBMISSIVE TO ALL, OBEDIENT TO GOD

God asks that we submit fully to one another, but He doesn't ask us to blindly obey others. We must first be obedient to God and everything that He says. We must do everything in agreement with this, but nothing that contradicts what God tells us to do. If we want to get to know who Jesus is, we need to bow before God in the areas of obedience and submission.

Without faith it is impossible to please God,
because anyone who comes to Him must believe
that He exists and that He rewards those
who earnestly seek Him.
Hebrews 11:6

"Abba, Father," He said, "everything is possible
for You. Take this cup from Me. Yet not what
I will, but what You will."
Mark 14:36

LOVE AND OBEDIENCE

To have a relationship with God means to love Him
and that means to obey Him. It's not possible to love
God and yet be continually disobedient. The greatest
blessing and fulfilment in life is to give yourself completely to God's love in obedience to Him.

Jesus said, "If you love Me, keep My commands.
And I will ask the Father, and He will give you
another advocate to help you and be with you forever."
John 14:15-16

In fact, this is love for God: to keep His commands.
And His commands are not burdensome, for
everyone born of God overcomes the world.
1 John 5:3-4

JESUS MAKES OBEDIENCE POSSIBLE

Jesus willingly submitted Himself to the Father and did everything the Father asked of Him, even when it cost Him His life. The willingness that Jesus requires from us does not differ from His own. Jesus not only requires perfect obedience from us, but He also makes it possible in the life of every believer.

Ask Jesus to help you to be obedient and in that way you will be a light that shines for Him through your actions and words.

Once made perfect, He became the source of eternal salvation for all who obey Him.

Hebrews 5:9

It is God who works in you to will and to act in order to fulfill His good purpose. Do everything without grumbling or arguing.

Philippians 2:13-14

FULLNESS OF LIFE

God is the Source of life, which means that complete obedience leads to fullness of life. Disobedience leads to death. Some people desire to have authority over others, but they themselves are not willing to submit to any authority.

The best qualification for being in a position of authority is for you to submit to God's authority. Then you will become a great leader.

Jesus said, "Very truly I tell you, whoever obeys My word will never see death."
Psalm John 8:51

I will always obey Your law, for ever and ever.
I will walk about in freedom, for I have sought out Your precepts.
Psalm 119:44-45

MODERN IDOL WORSHIP

To worship anything other than God or to obey any other is idolatry. God requires complete obedience and worship. When we follow our own will instead of God's, and no longer obey Him, we are being idolaters: We are obeying an authority other than God's. To worship God means to be obedient to Him.

Does the LORD delight in burnt offerings and sacrifices as much as in obeying the LORD? To obey is better than sacrifice, and to heed is better than the fat of rams. For rebellion is like the sin of divination, and arrogance like the evil of idolatry.
1 Samuel 15:22-23

To love Him with all your heart, with all your understanding and with all your strength, and to love your neighbor as yourself is more important than all burnt offerings and sacrifices.
Mark 12:33

THE THIEF OF JOY

Don't compare your circumstances with what happens to other believers. You must trust in God even though your life seems to be crumbling around you while other believers stand strong and victorious.

Make sure you stand pure and dedicated before God and don't compare yourself with others' successes or setbacks. Be sure that you are answering God's call to obedience – "Follow Me!"

Then Jesus said, "Follow Me!"
John 21:19

"Anyone who hears and doesn't obey is like a person who builds a house without a foundation. When the floods sweep down against that house, it will collapse into a heap of ruins."
Luke 6:49 NLT

THE CONSEQUENCE OF DISOBEDIENCE

Suffering can definitely be a consequence of disobedience. The reason for this is that any path away from God is sinful and lifeless and can only result in death. Obedience to God leads to Jesus. Ask God to help you to turn to Him in every path of disobedience that you are walking. He will lead you on the path of purity and true life.

But if He says, "I am not pleased with you," then I am ready; let Him do to me whatever seems good to Him.
2 Samuel 15:26

"Enter through the narrow gate. For wide is the gate and broad is the road that leads to destruction, and many enter through it. But small is the gate and narrow the road that leads to life, and only a few find it."
Matthew 7:13-14

A DAY IS COMING ...

There is no such thing as luck in a believer's life, therefore a date like Friday 13 holds no sway over us. But there is a day coming that is very ominous and that is the Day of Judgment. It has nothing to do with luck, fortune-telling or superstition. But what happens after this day can mean an eternity without Christ. Bow before the Lord and beg Him to forgive you so that you can spend eternity with Him.

> *"Many will say to Me on that day, 'Lord, Lord, did we not prophesy in Your name and in your name drive out demons and in Your name perform many miracles?' Then I will tell them plainly, 'I never knew you. Away from Me, you evildoers!'"*
> Matthew 7:22-23

> *Let no one be found among you who sacrifices their son or daughter in the fire, who practices divination or sorcery, interprets omens, engages in witchcraft, or casts spells, or who is a medium or spiritist or who consults the dead. Anyone who does these things is detestable to the LORD.*
> Deuteronomy 18:10-12

YOUR ALARM SYSTEM

Our conscience is our inborn alarm system that tells us whether something is right or wrong. God defines what is right and wrong, but sometimes our conscience doesn't align with God's will.

The Holy Spirit works through our conscience, but it can happen that we are so hardened that the Holy Spirit can't get through. Pray that God will help you to align your conscience with His will so that you can clearly hear the Holy Spirit when He warns you.

Paul looked straight at the Sanhedrin and said,
"My brothers, I have fulfilled my duty to God
in all good conscience to this day."
Acts 23:1

The one who keeps God's commands lives in Him,
and He in them. And this is how we know that He
lives in us: We know it by the Spirit He gave us.
1 John 3:24

FOUR KINDS OF CONSCIENCE

There are four kinds of conscience described in the Bible. The first one is in 1 Timothy 4:2, which says their consciences had been "seared as with a hot iron." First Corinthians 8:12 speaks of a "weak conscience" and 1 Timothy 1:5 describes a "good conscience." The fourth kind is a secular conscience that allows ungodly things because it thinks they are good. Inspect your conscience and make sure that it is pure and in keeping with God's will.

Whether you turn to the right or to the left, your ears will hear a voice behind you, saying, "This is the way; walk in it."
Isaiah 30:21

Cling to your faith in Christ, and keep your conscience clear. For some people have deliberately violated their consciences; as a result, their faith has been shipwrecked.
1 Timothy 1:19 NLT

JESUS HEALS A SEARED CONSCIENCE

We all have an "inner policeman" to help us to do right, but this policeman can be corrupt. The worst is a conscience that has been seared with a hot iron. In this instance, the policeman is so corrupt that he doesn't respond to any charges of bad behavior. When you don't do what you know is right, your conscience is numbed. Jesus, however, can restore a seared conscience and make it whole again if we would just come before Him in repentance.

The Spirit clearly says that in later times some will abandon the faith and follow deceiving spirits and things taught by demons. Such teachings come through hypocritical liars, whose consciences have been seared as with a hot iron.

1 Timothy 4:1-2

Watch your life and doctrine closely. Persevere in them, because if you do, you will save both yourself and your hearers.

1 Timothy 4:16

JESUS HEALS A WEAK CONSCIENCE

A weak conscience doesn't have the correct information and accuses the person of things for which they are not guilty. This causes conflict, because God's definition of right and wrong does not coincide with what the person thinks.

The Bible encourages those with a weak conscience to grow in Christ so that they can serve Him better. Learning man-made laws weakens our conscience, but the blood of Christ cleanses us from this.

When you sin against them in this way and wound their weak conscience, you sin against Christ.
1 Corinthians 8:12

In the same way, the Lord ordered that those who preach the Good News should be supported by those who benefit from it.
1 Corinthians 9:14 NLT

JESUS GIVES US A GOOD CONSCIENCE

A good conscience after you have been born again is one that is maintained by God and that knows what God considers right and wrong. This conscience does not grow by learning rules and laws, but is nurtured by the Holy Spirit who is present in every believer. A good conscience has a name: Jesus Christ. With Christ in our lives we can grow to be more like Him. He frees our consciences to serve God.

How much more, then, will the blood of Christ,
who through the eternal Spirit offered Himself
unblemished to God, cleanse our consciences
from acts that lead to death, so that we
may serve the living God!
Hebrews 9:14

The goal of this command is love, which comes
from a pure heart and a good conscience
and a sincere faith.
1 Timothy 1:5

EXERCISE A GOOD CONSCIENCE

A pure conscience is one that comes from Jesus and is exercised often. Just as you can numb your conscience, so too can you awaken it by doing what is right. In everyday life you will get opportunities to practice having a good and pure conscience. Every step of obedience brings you closer to Jesus.

*As for you, the anointing you received from Him remains
in you, and you do not need anyone to teach you.
But as His anointing teaches you about all things and
as that anointing is real, not counterfeit – just as
it has taught you, remain in Him.*
1 John 2:27

*What we have received is not the spirit of the world,
but the Spirit who is from God, so that we may
understand what God has freely given us.*
1 Corinthians 2:12

A PURER CONSCIENCE IN JESUS

You can determine God's will through getting to know Him better. The more you can discern God's will, the more mature and pure your conscience will become before God. This is a process that never ends. Ask God to help you to grow in your knowledge of Jesus so that your conscience becomes more pure.

Flee the evil desires of youth and pursue righteousness,
faith, love and peace, along with those who call
on the Lord out of a pure heart.
2 Timothy 2:22

Keep your conscience clear. Then if people speak
against you, they will be ashamed when they see what
a good life you live because you belong to Christ.
1 Peter 3:16 NLT

AN UNSAVED CONSCIENCE

The conscience you have before salvation is a defective one and has not yet been awakened by the life of Jesus Christ. It is one that is programmed by society and personal values. This kind of conscience undergoes a revolution after salvation because certain things are no longer acceptable according to God's standards. This conscience is no longer satisfied with self-justification, but with what is right in God's eyes.

Let us draw near to God with a sincere heart and with the full assurance that faith brings, having our hearts sprinkled to cleanse us from a guilty conscience and having our bodies washed with pure water. Let us hold unswervingly to the hope we profess, for He who promised is faithful.

Hebrews 10:22-23

To the pure all things are pure, but to those who are defiled and unbelieving nothing is pure; but even their mind and conscience are defiled.

Titus 1:15 NKJV

A BORN-AGAIN CONSCIENCE

A conscience that has been born again registers quickly that something is not right, even though it might be generally acceptable. This is because it has been awakened by God. For example, without anyone telling you, you know that your broken relationship with your parents isn't right. There is something that now drives you to make right that which previously didn't bother you. Jesus' life within you requires you to reflect God's truth in your life.

They show that the requirements of the law are written
on their hearts, their consciences also bearing witness,
and their thoughts sometimes accusing them and
at other times even defending them.
Romans 2:15

It is necessary to submit to the authorities, not
only because of possible punishment but also
as a matter of conscience.
Romans 13:5

YOU CAN'T BRIBE GOD

One can negotiate with God, but one cannot bribe God. Your conscience might bother you because you promised to do something if God helped you and now you haven't fulfilled your side of the deal. The only transaction that God entered into was through His Son. Jesus has already met all the requirements.

God doesn't help us because we make a deal with Him; He helps us because He wants to. All that God asks is that we obey His Son.

You are a chosen people. You are royal priests,
a holy nation, God's very own possession. As a
result, you can show others the goodness of
God, for He called you out of the darkness
into His wonderful light.
1 Peter 2:9

I have considered my ways and have turned my
steps to your statutes. I will hasten and not
delay to obey Your commands.
Psalm 119:59-60

GOD'S HIGHEST PRIORITY

Sometimes we make it look like we want to obey God, but we don't really. We will do anything except forgive and respect our parents, or mix with society's underdogs or pray for the government.

We *must* understand that the greatest fulfilment lies in doing what is on God's heart, what is important to Him.

Now that you have purified yourselves by obeying the truth so that you have sincere love for each other, love one another deeply, from the heart.
1 Peter 1:22

Dear friends, let us love one another, for love comes from God. Everyone who loves has been born of God and knows God. Whoever does not love does not know God, because God is love.
1 John 4:7-8

MUST WE ALWAYS OBEY?

Obedience has got to do with submission to authority. However, there is a time and place when we might be called to disobey that authority. This could happen when obedience to what people are telling us to do would mean disobedience to God.

We might have to bear the cost of disobedience to authority, but obedience to God at the cost of our lives demonstrates Jesus' victory over Satan.

Do what is right and good in the LORD's sight, so that
it may go well with you and you may go in and take
over the good land the LORD promised on
oath to your ancestors.
Deuteronomy 6:18

I hold fast to Your statutes, LORD;
do not let me be put to shame. I run in
the path of Your commands, for You have
broadened my understanding.
Psalm 119:31-32

HONOR YOUR PARENTS

God desires us to respect and honor our parents, even when they don't deserve it. Everything in our world is conditional – love, respect, obedience – while everything in God's kingdom is unconditional. To honor our parents regardless of their lifestyle or behavior is to be obedient to Almighty God. When we are obedient we will have access to God's heart and that will bring us blessing and fulfilment.

*"Honor your father and your mother, so that you may live long in the land the L*ORD *your God is giving you."*

Exodus 20:12

"Honor your father and mother." This is the first commandment with a promise: If you honor your father and mother, "things will go well for you, and you will have a long life on the earth."

Ephesians 6:2-3 NLT

GODLESSNESS

Why does wickedness continue; why doesn't God put a stop to it? The answer is simple: The workers of iniquity are zealous and loyal to their master while the rest are still deciding where their loyalty lies. Few of us want to sacrifice for the greater good, namely God's sovereignty and rule over man.

We must pray that God will remove the divisions, disputes and lack of unity between believers so that we can obey Him and oppose the godlessness in the world.

He will give justice to the poor and make fair decisions for the exploited. The earth will shake at the force of His word, and one breath from His mouth will destroy the wicked.
Isaiah 11:4 NLT

Praise the LORD! How joyful are those who fear the LORD and delight in obeying His commands.
Psalm 112:1 NLT

DISGUISING YOUR SINS

In God's perfect holiness every form of evil is painfully obvious. We try to disguise our sins with words such as "white lies" and "everyone is doing it," but in the presence of God the true wickedness of our sin stands out. The only reaction for our disobedience from God is judgment. Bow before God and ask Him to forgive you for your sins and help you to be obedient to Him so that you can once again stand in His presence.

For all have sinned and fall short
of the glory of God.
Romans 3:23

Praise the LORD, my soul; all my inmost being, praise
His holy name. Praise the LORD, my soul, and forget not
all His benefits – who forgives all your sins and heals
all your diseases, who redeems your life from the pit
and crowns you with love and compassion.
Psalm 103:1-4

A FINANCIAL GOSPEL?

It is important to distinguish between "obeying" and "giving," because to obey God doesn't always mean to give money. Many churches trick people by their definition of obeying and giving. God is not stingy and He doesn't manipulate people. He loves people. Stay in tune with God's will and be obedient to Him, not to the financial gospel that others preach.

For I resolved to know nothing while I was with
you except Jesus Christ and Him crucified.
1 Corinthians 2:2

What is more, I consider everything a loss because of
the surpassing worth of knowing Christ Jesus my Lord,
for whose sake I have lost all things. I consider them
garbage, that I may gain Christ.
Philippians 3:8

GOD EXALTS THE OBEDIENT

Those who are exalted by God will admit in their hearts that it is sometimes difficult to obey Him, but they do it in any case. They forgive instead of taking revenge. In this, Jesus is our example when He said of His accusers, "Father, forgive them, for they do not know what they are doing" (Luke 23:34). If we remain obedient to God, He will exalt us at the right time.

"But I tell you, love your enemies and pray for those who persecute you."
Matthew 5:44

"I gave them this command: Obey Me, and I will be your God and you will be My people. Walk in obedience to all I command you, that it may go well with you."
Jeremiah 7:23

SERVING THE LORD

We are in desperate need of those who are willing to obey God, even though it might anger their families. These are people who will love even when no one agrees with them and submit to God even though no one else does. We have a need for people who will say, as Joshua did, "As for me and my house, we will serve the Lord." The question is, what are we willing to sacrifice in order to obey God?

"But if serving the Lord seems undesirable to you, then choose for yourselves this day whom you will serve, whether the gods your ancestors served beyond the Euphrates, or the gods of the Amorites, in whose land you are living. But as for me and my household, we will serve the Lord."

Joshua 24:15

Then Jesus said to His disciples, "Whoever wants to be My disciple must deny themselves and take up their cross and follow Me."

Matthew 16:24

LET YOUR LIGHT SHINE

Obedience to God and loving those who might not deserve it are the way we reflect God's goodness and love to the world. If we are obedient to God and submit to Him we will be the salt and light to a world in desperate need of a Savior.

"In the same way, let your light shine before others, that they may see your good deeds and glorify your Father in heaven."
Matthew 5:16

"You are the salt of the earth. But if the salt loses its saltiness, how can it be made salty again? It is no longer good for anything, except to be thrown out and trampled underfoot."
Matthew 5:13

For you were once darkness, but now you are light in the Lord. Live as children of light.
Ephesians 5:8

OCTOBER

FISHERS OF MEN

"Come, follow Me," Jesus said, "and I will send you out to fish for people." At once they left their nets and followed Him. Matthew 4:19-20

DON'T PUT PEOPLE ON A PEDESTAL

It's interesting how some people treat pastors. Some treat them quite disparagingly, while others treat them as if they are God. They will swear and gossip in front of Jesus, but never in front of the pastor. Pastors are just people, also in need of salvation. Beware of placing people above God.

"Don't let anyone call you 'Rabbi,' for you have only one teacher, and all of you are equal as brothers and sisters. And don't address anyone here on earth as 'Father,' for only God in heaven is your spiritual Father. And don't let anyone call you 'Teacher,' for you have only one teacher, the Messiah. The greatest among you must be a servant. But those who exalt themselves will be humbled, and those who humble themselves will be exalted."

Matthew 23:8-12 NLT

JESUS IS GREATER

Jesus is greater than any prophet or servant of God. He is greater than any pastor or church. We sometimes focus so much on people and what they do that we forget they are sinners just like us. It's time we focus on Jesus and start to live as He did.

Jesus has been found worthy of greater honor than Moses, just as the builder of a house has greater honor than the house itself.

Hebrews 3:3

Friends, why are you doing this? We too are only human, like you. We are bringing you good news, telling you to turn from these worthless things to the living God, who made the heavens and the earth and the sea and everything in them.

Acts 14:15

GREAT EXPECTATIONS

Jesus commanded His disciples to be like Him. If this is impossible, how can He expect us to do so? The truth is that Jesus was not unreasonable; He knew what He was talking about (see John 3:11). Religious people cannot be like Jesus. Only those who are renewed through God's Spirit can be like Him. No ordinary person can get rid of sin, but disciples of Jesus can. A person *can* be like Jesus – if God has made you made new, then "all things are possible."

When the disciples heard this, they were greatly astonished and asked, "Who then can be saved?" Jesus looked at them and said, "With man this is impossible, but with God all things are possible."
Matthew 19:25-26

This will continue until we all come to such unity in our faith and knowledge of God's Son that we will be mature in the Lord, measuring up to the full and complete standard of Christ.
Ephesians 4:13 NLT

MORE LIKE JESUS

To be like Jesus doesn't mean that we become God or that we are flawless and divinely perfect. It means that we grow to be more like Jesus. We all have the ability to live like Jesus, but we have to work at it. If you don't believe it is possible to be like Jesus, then you are either not born again or you don't understand God's truth. Don't say that you can't live like you should. Ask God to fulfill His purpose for you so that you can become more like Jesus.

Dear friends, let us love one another,
for love comes from God. Everyone who
loves has been born of God and knows God.
1 John 4:7

"Be perfect, therefore, as
your heavenly Father is perfect."
Matthew 5:48

ARE YOU RIGHTEOUS?

If someone stood up in church and said that they were just as righteous as Jesus, how would you react? Is it blasphemy or is it the truth? John says that if we live righteously we are righteous, just as God is righteous. This means to stand before God without guilt or condemnation. Is this possible? John gives us the answer in his letter …

The one who does what is right is righteous,
just as He is righteous.
1 John 3:7

If we confess our sins, He is faithful and just and
will forgive us our sins and purify us from
all unrighteousness.
1 John 1:9

DECIDE TO FOLLOW JESUS

To be a Christian means that you are a disciple of Jesus – someone who follows Him. This is what the word *Christian* means. Either I am lord over my life or Jesus is Lord. It is one or the other. I can't be lord of my life and follow Jesus at the same time. Where do you stand? Ask Jesus to be the highest authority in your life and serve Him in truth and deed.

Yet to all who did receive Him, to those who believed in His name, He gave the right to become children of God – children born not of natural descent, nor of human decision or a husband's will, but born of God.

John 1:12-13

However, if you suffer as a Christian, do not be ashamed, but praise God that you bear that name.

1 Peter 4:16

TO BE LIKE JESUS

Imagine being a fly on the wall in Jerusalem when twelve-year-old Jesus sat talking to the religious leaders! The reaction of the learned men shows that Jesus wasn't a smart aleck, but a sincere child (see Luke 2:47). His wisdom and insight into Scripture impressed them immensely. As a result of His nature, Jesus "grew in wisdom and stature, and in favor with God and man" (Luke 2:52). Do you want to be like Jesus? Pray and ask God so that you would grow in favor with Him.

And we all, who with unveiled faces contemplate the Lord's glory, are being transformed into His image with ever-increasing glory, which comes from the Lord, who is the Spirit.

2 Corinthians 3:18

"I have set you an example that you should do as I have done for you."

John 13:15

ARE YOU HUMBLE?

To be humble means to agree with God, since agreeing with Him is a character trait of the Holy Spirit. If we can say we are patient, friendly and long-suffering, then we also need to be able to say that we are humble. There is a need for humble people. Jesus shows us the way, the best example of humility for us to follow.

Always be humble and gentle. Be patient with each other, making allowance for each other's faults because of your love. Make every effort to keep yourselves united in the Spirit, binding yourselves together with peace.
Ephesians 4:2-3 NLT

We prove ourselves by our purity, our understanding, our patience, our kindness, by the Holy Spirit within us, and by our sincere love.
2 Corinthians 6:6 NLT

OUR GREATEST JOY

True humility is the recognition that you are worthy, not because of your piety, appearance or self-worth, but because you are the crown of God's creation. Jesus knew this and lived joyfully with this knowledge. Jesus is the perfect example of someone who agrees with God on everything – the perfect example of humility. Our greatest joy lies in living in agreement with God.

Make me truly happy by agreeing wholeheartedly with each other, loving one another, and working together with one mind and purpose. Don't be selfish; don't try to impress others. Be humble, thinking of others as better than yourselves.
Philippians 2:2-3 NLT

Pride leads to disgrace, but with humility comes wisdom.
Proverbs 11:2 NLT

ACHIEVEMENTS AREN'T EVERYTHING

People who measure their worth based on their achievements are foolish. This kind of success goes against everything that God says and does. If we measure our worth by our achievements, then we will apply the same measure to those around us. There are many people sitting in church who feel they "have arrived," which can be seen in the way they treat others. These people don't understand Jesus. Believers who can see through God's eyes find it easy to love as God loves.

Live in harmony with one another. Do not be proud,
but be willing to associate with people of low position.
Do not be conceited.
Romans 12:16

Therefore, as God's chosen people, holy and dearly
loved, clothe yourselves with compassion, kindness,
humility, gentleness and patience.
Colossians 3:12

BEHAVIOR AND CHARACTER

God's primary focus is not on correct behavior, but on an honorable character. This doesn't mean that God doesn't care about behavior. We tend to focus on behavior, while God focuses on character. We often want to do the right thing, even if it's not with our whole heart. We do things that display the right behavior, but our hearts are not bowed before God. Pray that the Father would help you to grow in Jesus so that you can reflect Him in your life.

If anyone obeys His word, love for God is made complete in them. This is how we know we are in Him: Whoever claims to live in Him must live as Jesus did.

1 John 2:5-6

Follow my example, as I follow the example of Christ.

1 Corinthians 11:1

WHO ARE YOU IN THE DARK?

Character is who you are when no one else is watching. Character is reflected in behavior, but good behavior does not necessarily mean good character. Correct behavior can be learned without it coming from the heart. God wants to teach you to have a new character, out of which the right behavior will automatically flow. Stop focusing on behavior and rather focus on God so that He can teach you good character.

You were taught, with regard to your former way of life, to put off your old self, which is being corrupted by its deceitful desires; to be made new in the attitude of your minds; and to put on the new self, created to be like God in true righteousness and holiness. Therefore each of you must put off falsehood and speak truthfully to your neighbor, for we are all members of one body.

Ephesians 4:22-25

BEHAVIOR SHAPED BY CHARACTER

From childhood we are taught what good behavior is. This isn't wrong, but it is misleading because it can create the impression that a person is pious, even though it may not necessarily be true. Our attempts to live holy lives have to do with our behavior, without allowing the character of Christ to grow in us. The truth is that it is Jesus' character from which all holy and uplifting behavior springs.

"Everything they do is done for people to see: They make their phylacteries wide and the tassels on their garments long."
Matthew 23:5

Follow God's example, therefore, as dearly loved children and walk in the way of love, just as Christ loved us and gave Himself up for us as a fragrant offering and sacrifice to God.
Ephesians 5:1-2

TRUE WORSHIP

Jesus accused the Pharisees of having a relationship with God that was built on man-made laws and not on true worship. Even today some people want to worship God, but on their own terms that make worship easy and convenient. The best way to see what man-made laws you've learned and applied to your own life is to measure them against the Person and character of Jesus. If it differs, throw it out.

"They worship Me in vain; their teachings are merely human rules."

Mark 7:7

"Yet a time is coming and has now come when the true worshipers will worship the Father in the Spirit and in truth, for they are the kind of worshipers the Father seeks."

John 4:23

ROOTED IN CHRIST

To walk with Jesus means to live in Him. The words *in Jesus* mean "like Him," "as He would have it" and "as He gives power." A disciple does what his Master does. There is only one way of being a disciple of Jesus and walking with Him and that is to be rooted in Jesus. To be rooted in Jesus is easy. It means that He rules over your whole life. How do you do this? By focusing on His teachings and obeying Him.

So then, just as you received Christ Jesus as Lord, continue to live your lives in Him, rooted and built up in Him, strengthened in the faith as you were taught, and overflowing with thankfulness.
Colossians 2:6-7

He refreshes my soul. He guides me along the right paths for His name's sake.
Psalm 23:3

FOCUS ON JESUS

To live in Jesus means you must stay focused on Him. This is the only way to walk with the Lord and to be built up in the Spirit. There is no lasting support or encouragement outside of Jesus. Stay rooted in Christ!

We do this by keeping our eyes on Jesus, the champion who initiates and perfects our faith. Because of the joy awaiting Him, He endured the cross, disregarding its shame. Now He is seated in the place of honor beside God's throne.

Hebrews 12:2 NLT

You will keep in perfect peace those whose minds are steadfast, because they trust in You. Trust in the LORD, forever, for the LORD, the LORD Himself, is the Rock eternal.

Isaiah 26:3-4

LIVE LIKE JESUS

The strongest testimony believers have is how they live in front of others. To talk about Jesus is one thing, and it is very important, but to demonstrate Him is far more important because it adds integrity to what you say. Be a witness for Jesus today by the way you live your life.

Be careful to live properly among your unbelieving neighbors. Then even if they accuse you of doing wrong, they will see your honorable behavior, and they will give honor to God when He judges the world.
1 Peter 2:12 NLT

He must also have a good reputation with outsiders, so that he will not fall into disgrace and into the devil's trap.
1 Timothy 3:7

THE BEST WITNESS

Our lives and relationships are the strongest witness we can give. How will people know you submit to God's authority if they don't see it in your actions and how you treat other people? It is such a disappointment when someone talks about Jesus in their lives, but acts in a contradictory way. True disciples live in accordance to what they say, otherwise they have nothing to talk about.

"You will receive power when the Holy Spirit comes on you; and you will be My witnesses in Jerusalem, and in all Judea and Samaria, and to the ends of the earth."

Acts 1:8

"In the same way, let your light shine before others, that they may see your good deeds and glorify your Father in heaven."

Matthew 5:16

AN IMPORTANT PART TO PLAY

The gospel and truth of Jesus penetrates all sectors of society. When Jesus was on earth, He was a man in bodily form. However, on earth today, Christ Jesus lives in a million places. He lives among people through the lives of His disciples. Where Jesus' disciples are, He is. So even though we are just a small piece of the big picture, we each have a significant part to play.

You will be His witness to all people of
what you have seen and heard.
Acts 22:15

A truthful witness saves lives, but a
false witness is deceitful.
Proverbs 14:25

AN OPEN LETTER

All Jesus' disciples are in full-time service, regardless of what job they do. We are an open letter of God's saving grace and glory that can be read by anyone. Through us, Jesus' holiness breaks like waves over the earth. In our lifetime we not only see God work mightily in our lives, but also in the lives of others.

Preach the word; be prepared in season and out of season; correct, rebuke and encourage – with great patience and careful instruction.
2 Timothy 4:2

Oh, the depth of the riches of the wisdom and knowledge of God! How unsearchable His judgments, and His paths beyond tracing out!
Romans 11:33

ACCEPTED IN CHRIST

We do not deserve God's acceptance – we receive it for free. We receive so much from God that we feel an obligation to share it with others. We must take the acceptance we receive from God and give it to others without keeping a record of it. This begins when we pray, and God's love and acceptance wash over us and those around us. It is in this light that we see the necessity of Jesus' service in the world and how scarce it sometimes is.

… So that you may become blameless and pure,
"children of God without fault in a warped and
crooked generation." Then you will shine among
them like stars in the sky as you hold
firmly to the word of life.
Philippians 2:15-16

Let us not become weary in doing good, for at
the proper time we will reap a harvest if
we do not give up.
Galatians 6:9

JESUS GIVES LIFE IN ABUNDANCE

Jesus gives life in abundance, but when we find it lacking it is because we never asked for it and received it. When Jesus gives, He gives in abundance so that we can share with others. He makes us the distributors of His glory. To be served by Jesus is the key to change that is lasting and filled with joy.

All this is from God, who reconciled us to Himself through Christ and gave us the ministry of reconciliation: that God was reconciling the world to Himself in Christ, not counting people's sins against them. And He has committed us to the message of reconciliation.

2 Corinthians 5:18-19

Be sure to fear the LORD and serve Him faithfully with all your heart; consider what great things He has done for you.

1 Samuel 12:24

MISSIONS

The word *missions* doesn't always get a positive response from people because they have a wrong understanding of what it is. Missions has to do with Jesus: He tells us that we have received life in abundance and that we must share it. It doesn't matter if you share Jesus' abundance with your family, colleagues, neighbors, or strangers in a foreign land. It doesn't matter where it is as long as there are people who need life in abundance.

Whatever you do, work at it with all your heart,
as working for the Lord, not for human masters.
Colossians 3:23

Don't let anyone look down on you because you are
young, but set an example for the believers in speech,
in conduct, in love, in faith and in purity.
1 Timothy 4:12

YOU CAN BE A MISSIONARY

Missions is not just something that happens far away with a few people. God loves all people and wants everyone to come to salvation. If we don't understand missions in this way, then we don't understand Jesus' ministry. Jesus calls us to freely give what we have freely received – everywhere and to everyone. Are you ready to be a missionary?

Then Peter began to speak: "I now realize how true it is that God does not show favoritism but accepts from every nation the one who fears Him and does what is right."
Acts 10:34-35

There is neither Jew nor Gentile, neither slave nor free, nor is there male and female, for you are all one in Christ Jesus.
Galatians 3:28

WITNESS WHERE YOU ARE

According to God, the "missionary kind of people" are those who are obedient. You can't choose whether you are the missionary kind or not. Jesus gives us the command to be His witnesses. Who must do it? Is anyone excluded? The only people who are excluded are unbelievers because they are not in Jesus. If you are a disciple of Jesus, then He has given you the command to be a witness for Him.

> *"Therefore go and make disciples of all nations, baptizing them in the name of the Father and of the Son and of the Holy Spirit."*
> *Matthew 28:19*

> *"You are the light of the world. A town built on a hill cannot be hidden. Neither do people light a lamp and put it under a bowl. Instead they put it on its stand, and it gives light to everyone in the house."*
> *Matthew 5:14-15*

ACTIONS SPEAK LOUDER THAN WORDS

One of Jesus' main tasks was to establish the disciples' faith in who He was. They believed in Him as a teacher, but did they believe in Him as the King and Lord of the universe? Do you believe that Jesus is who He says He is and can do everything He says He can? Our answer is revealed in our everyday behavior. The people around us will clearly see what we think of Him.

For this very reason, make every effort to add to your faith goodness; and to goodness, knowledge; and to knowledge, self-control; and to self-control, perseverance; and to perseverance, godliness; and to godliness, mutual affection; and to mutual affection, love.

2 Peter 1:5-7

Worship Christ as Lord of your life. And if someone asks you about your hope as a believer, always be ready to explain it.

1 Peter 3:15 NLT

WHO DO YOU SAY HE IS?

Some people think that Jesus is relevant for spiritual situations and discussions, but not for practical everyday living. Jesus is for church and saying grace at meals and that is it. As He did with His disciples, Jesus asks us today, "Who do you say I am?" (Matthew 16:15). Ask God to help you to show the world who He is by how you live your life.

"Now we can see that You know all things and that You do not even need to have anyone ask You questions. This makes us believe that You came from God." "Do you now believe?" Jesus replied.

John 16:30-31

Martha answered, "I know he will rise again in the resurrection at the last day." Jesus said to her, "I am the resurrection and the life. The one who believes in Me will live, even though they die."

John 11:24-25

THROUGH WORDS AND DEEDS

Jesus' disciples were left with many impressions and memories of their Lord. Teachings, dissertations and discussions are one thing, but how we live our lives is something else. Jesus set a perfect example and His disciples got to understand Him through His teachings, but also by how He conducted Himself. Jesus' life permeated the disciples' lives – their behavior, speech, thoughts and relationships. Their preaching demonstrated the way they lived. The same should be true of us today as we attempt to be fishers of men.

Above all, love each other deeply, because love covers over a multitude of sins.
1 Peter 4:8

To this you were called, because Christ suffered for you, leaving you an example, that you should follow in His steps.
1 Peter 2:21

FOLLOW JESUS

The word *disciple* has become distorted in our world today. It has come to mean something academic and theoretical, something abstract and philosophical. But Jesus was completely different. He was the most spiritual Person to ever live, setting the example for us to follow. Would the way you live your life fit in with Jesus and His disciples?

Let the message of Christ dwell among you richly as you teach and admonish one another with all wisdom through psalms, hymns, and songs from the Spirit, singing to God with gratitude in your hearts. And whatever you do, whether in word or deed, do it all in the name of the Lord Jesus, giving thanks to God the Father through Him.

Colossians 3:16-17

Jesus said, "You are truly My disciples if you remain faithful to My teachings."

John 8:31

BELIEVERS ARE EQUAL

Many people are told never to challenge the pastor, because they are God's anointed. The truth is that all believers are anointed – all believers have Almighty God dwelling in them. Those in the church are responsible before God for every word and deed, and the attitude they display towards others. We mustn't put one believer on a pedestal above the others. Rather, we must recognize some as being more spiritually mature than others.

Don't lord it over the people assigned to your care, but lead them by your own good example.
1 Peter 5:3 NLT

But you are not like that, for you are a chosen people. You are royal priests, a holy nation, God's very own possession. As a result, you can show others the goodness of God, for He called you out of the darkness into His wonderful light.
1 Peter 2:9 NLT

TRUE SPIRITUALITY

God's definition of true spiritually starts with Jesus … always Jesus. He is the most spiritual Person to ever walk the earth. He is the perfect example for anyone wanting to fulfil God's definition of spirituality. To be like Jesus is to be truly spiritual.

The fruit of the Spirit is love, joy, peace, forbearance,
kindness, goodness, faithfulness, gentleness and
self-control. Against such things there is no law.
Those who belong to Christ Jesus have crucified
the flesh with its passions and desires.
Galatians 5:22-24

"By their fruit you will recognize them. Do people
pick grapes from thornbushes, or figs from thistles?
Likewise, every good tree bears good fruit, but a
bad tree bears bad fruit."
Matthew 7:16-17

NOVEMBER

SAILING STRONG

Be on guard. Stand firm in the faith.
Be courageous. Be strong. 1 Corinthians 16:13 NLT

TRANSFORMED INTO HIS IMAGE

In 2 Corinthians, Paul says that the most natural thing for born-again believers is to be like Jesus, because the same Spirit that is in Jesus is also in us. Born-again children of God have one great ambition: to grow in Christ. This isn't possible for other people. Through salvation, Jesus has freed you to be just like Him. You can now sail ahead through strong gales because Jesus is with you, making your character like His.

And we all, who with unveiled faces contemplate the Lord's glory, are being transformed into His image with ever-increasing glory, which comes from the Lord, who is the Spirit.

2 Corinthians 3:18

Until we all reach unity in the faith and in the knowledge of the Son of God and become mature, attaining to the whole measure of the fullness of Christ.

Ephesians 4:13

A DIVINE NATURE

Peter teaches us that when we are born-again, we are freed from the world and we receive the divine nature. Jesus is the One who makes this possible; through Him we receive His nature. If we aren't born again, we try to live good and moral lives without success. Turn to God and ask Him to cleanse your heart so that you can live according to His will.

Through these He has given us His very great and precious promises, so that through them you may participate in the divine nature, having escaped the corruption in the world caused by evil desires.

2 Peter 1:4

They disciplined us for a little while as they thought best; but God disciplines us for our good, in order that we may share in His holiness.

Hebrews 12:10

LIVING AS JESUS DID

If we aren't born again, we can't be like Jesus. If the Spirit of Christ doesn't make us new, then the life of God is not in us. If the life of God is in us, we live through God; and if we live through God, we live His life. Religious people don't belong to this group, only born-again believers.

In fact, this is love for God: to keep His commands. And His commands are not burdensome, for everyone born of God overcomes the world. This is the victory that has overcome the world, even our faith.

1 John 5:3-4

Thanks be to God! He gives us the victory through our Lord Jesus Christ.

1 Corinthians 15:57

A CHANGED NATURE

A sinner is someone who has a sinful nature and who is cursed by God from the beginning (see Ephesians 2:3). All people enter the world this way, but not all people depart from earth in this manner. Some people have a change of heart and are made new in the nature of God.

It is because of Him that you are in Christ Jesus, who has become for us wisdom from God – that is, our righteousness, holiness and redemption.
1 Corinthians 1:30

But God showed His great love for us by sending Christ to die for us while we were still sinners. And since we have been made right in God's sight by the blood of Christ, He will certainly save us from God's condemnation.
Romans 5:8-9 NLT

OPEN THE DOOR

Jesus doesn't just open the door of your heart and walk in. He will only enter if you invite Him in. You have the choice whether to invite Him in or not. The same God who gave a choice to Adam and Eve is the same God who gives you a choice today. When Jesus enters our hearts, He has communion with us and there is intimacy. From this intimacy flows God's power, wisdom, life and love. Have you heard the Lord knocking on your door?

"Here I am! I stand at the door and knock.
If anyone hears My voice and opens the door,
I will come in and eat with that person,
and they with Me."
Revelation 3:20

To all who did receive Him, to those who
believed in His name, He gave the right to
become children of God.
John 1:12

WALK WITH THE LORD

People who grow in Christ grow in their submission to the Father. There is no other way to be spiritually mature. Everyone who walks in Jesus' steps walks in the blessings and glory of the Father. As the old hymn says, "When we walk with the Lord in the light of His word, what a glory He sheds on our way!" (John H. Sammis).

Grow in the grace and knowledge of our
Lord and Savior Jesus Christ. To Him be glory
both now and forever! Amen.
2 Peter 3:18

Neither the one who plants nor the one who waters
is anything, but only God, who makes things grow.
The one who plants and the one who waters have
one purpose, and they will each be rewarded
according to their own labor.
1 Corinthians 3:7-8

A CLEAN HEART

Being born again is the key to God. You can't carry out God's instructions if you aren't born again. As a born-again believer, God's nature is in you and you have the ability to do His will. Do you desire to live a holy life? Bow before God and ask Him to make your heart clean.

They are reborn – not with a physical birth resulting from human passion or plan, but a birth that comes from God.
John 1:13 NLT

Jesus replied, "Very truly I tell you, no one can see the kingdom of God unless they are born again."
John 3:3

SPIRITUAL FOOD

When we are born again, we receive God's nature. As with all new-borns, a process of growth has to occur before maturity can be reached. It is the same with our spiritual lives. We receive Christ's nature when we are born again and the process of spiritual growth lies ahead of us. In order to grow, we need to obey God. It doesn't help to chew our spiritual food and not swallow it – we will never be nourished this way.

*Through these He has given us His very great
and precious promises, so that through them you
may participate in the divine nature, having escaped
the corruption in the world caused by evil desires.*
2 Peter 1:4

*Jesus replied, "Anyone who loves Me will obey
My teaching. My Father will love them, and We will
come to them and make Our home with them."*
John 14:23

A SHINING LIGHT

God's definition of spirituality does not involve robes, rituals or ceremonies. God's definition is love – to love as Jesus did. This means He expects mercy rather than sacrifice (see Matthew 9:13). When you understand spirituality and the Christian life in these terms, then "your light will break forth like the dawn, and your healing will quickly appear; then your righteousness will go before you, and the glory of the LORD will be your rear guard" (Isaiah 58:8).

"Go and learn what this means: 'I desire mercy, not sacrifice.' For I have not come to call the righteous, but sinners."
Matthew 9:13

Is this the kind of fast I have chosen, only a day for people to humble themselves? Is it only for bowing one's head like a reed and for lying in sackcloth and ashes? Is that what you call a fast, a day acceptable to the LORD?
Isaiah 58:5

SPIRITUAL WARFARE

Spiritual warfare is the only truly holy war that can be engaged in. This war is not between people, but against the evil forces that want to destroy them. Spiritual warfare means to withstand Satan as he tries to use people to do his work. Jesus' disciples have a unique ability to put a stop to Satan's plans. Having Jesus in you makes you able to destroy the works of the evil one.

For our struggle is not against flesh and blood, but against the rulers, against the authorities, against the powers of this dark world and against the spiritual forces of evil in the heavenly realms.

Ephesians 6:12

Since the children have flesh and blood, He too shared in their humanity so that by His death He might break the power of him who holds the power of death – that is, the devil.

Hebrews 2:14

VICTORY OVER SATAN

Believers have an exceptional gift to engage in warfare with Satan and this is "the hope of glory." Any obedience to God, no matter how small, is part of effective spiritual warfare. Jesus' victory penetrates into society through every disciple's life, no matter how old or young they may be.

To them God has chosen to make known among the Gentiles the glorious riches of this mystery, which is Christ in you, the hope of glory.
Colossians 1:27

Be strong in the Lord and in His mighty power. Put on the full armor of God, so that you can take your stand against the devil's schemes.
Ephesians 6:10-11

WE ARE THE LORD'S ARMY

Spiritual warfare is not only meant for the experts and specialists. Every believer is called upon to take part in this warfare every day. Jesus is the expert and He fights this battle through us. There are no special armies to fight at the defense lines; we fight the battle in our everyday lives.

For though we live in the world, we do not wage war as the world does. The weapons we fight with are not the weapons of the world. On the contrary, they have divine power to demolish strongholds.

2 Corinthians 10:3-4

Stay alert! Watch out for your great enemy, the devil. He prowls around like a roaring lion, looking for someone to devour.

1 Peter 5:8 NLT

JESUS IS OUR ARMOR

Every day, all believers are involved in spiritual war-fare in some way or another. The most effective way to engage in this battle is to put on the armor of God. Every piece of armor reveals truths about Christ and no victory over the devil is possible without Him. The armor of God is nothing other than Jesus, and when the Son is honored through obedience, His victory takes place in our lives.

Stand firm then, with the belt of
truth buckled around your waist, with the
breastplate of righteousness in place, and
with your feet fitted with the readiness that
comes from the gospel of peace. In addition to
this, take up the shield of faith, with which
you can extinguish all the flaming
arrows of the evil one.
Ephesians 6:14-16

The light shines in the darkness, and the
darkness has not overcome it.
John 1:5

A NEW LIFE IN CHRIST

When you are born again you might find the following things apply to you: You hunger and thirst for the living Word of God and you get excited about God's authority. You have an intense desire to do God's will and feel a strong urge to forgive and reconcile with others. Meeting with other believers is satisfying because they speak your language and you start doing things you know God wants you to do, even though it might raise a few eyebrows.

Now that you have purified yourselves by obeying the truth so that you have sincere love for each other, love one another deeply, from the heart. For you have been born again, not of perishable seed, but of imperishable, through the living and enduring word of God.
1 Peter 1:22-23

A LIVING RELATIONSHIP WITH GOD

The most important way to know whether you are born again is the experience of knowing that you have personal contact with the living God and that you can hear and understand His voice. There is suddenly a clear understanding of God and His Word that wasn't there before. It isn't possible to be made new by God and not know about it. Salvation is real, relevant and for everyone.

Like newborn babies, crave pure spiritual milk, so that by it you may grow up in your salvation.

1 Peter 2:2

We were therefore buried with Him through baptism into death in order that, just as Christ was raised from the dead through the glory of the Father, we too may live a new life.

Romans 6:4

AM I STILL SAVED?

If the signs of being born again are no longer there, does it mean that you are no longer saved? There are three reasons you can use to evaluate yourself: The worries of life might drag you down; emotional baggage and unanswered questions can make you feel like you are no longer in touch with God; and a lack of contact with other believers can make you feel lost and alone. The initial signs that you are born again might make way for more mature signs of the divine life within you. You don't lose your salvation just because you don't feel saved.

In fact, though by this time you ought to be teachers, you need someone to teach you the elementary truths of God's word all over again. You need milk, not solid food!
Hebrews 5:12

I gave you milk, not solid food, for you were not yet ready for it. Indeed, you are still not ready.
1 Corinthians 3:2

FROM A CATERPILLAR TO A BUTTERFLY

You can change your circumstances in order to escape your problems, and for a while it can go well, but then all the old baggage returns because the problem is in your heart. We can't change our lives; only Jesus can. When we focus intently on our Almighty God, He transforms us from a caterpillar into a butterfly as He conforms us to His image. Do you feel like a lowly caterpillar? Allow Jesus to transform you into a butterfly. Just keep your eyes on Him.

And we all, who with unveiled faces contemplate the Lord's glory, are being transformed into His image with ever-increasing glory, which comes from the Lord, who is the Spirit.

2 Corinthians 3:18

For those God foreknew He also predestined to be conformed to the image of His Son, that He might be the firstborn among many brothers and sisters.

Romans 8:29

SAY NO TO THE WORLD

We are pressurized from all sides to reject our faith in Jesus Christ as our Lord and Savior. Jesus warns us not to give our life to the world, because then we will lose everything. However, if we lose our life for Christ's sake, then we will save it. Don't be blinded by the world's charm, because no temporary satisfaction is worth the cost of your soul.

"What will it profit a man if he gains the whole world, and loses his own soul? Or what will a man give in exchange for his soul?"
Mark 8:36-37 NKJV

"Whoever tries to keep their life will lose it, and whoever loses their life will preserve it."
Luke 17:33

DON'T SELL YOUR SOUL

Every day we are tempted to exchange irreplaceable things with replaceable ones. Every day people trade their souls for trivialities. We need to remember that a wise person gives what he cannot keep to gain what he cannot lose (Jim Elliot).

If we deliberately keep on sinning after we have received the knowledge of the truth, no sacrifice for sins is left, but only a fearful expectation of judgment and of raging fire that will consume the enemies of God.
Hebrews 10:26-27

"Do not be afraid of those who kill the body but cannot kill the soul. Rather, be afraid of the One who can destroy both soul and body in hell."
Matthew 10:28

SET AN EXAMPLE

Paul encourages believers to live a good life "so that your daily life may win the respect of outsiders and so that you will not be dependent on anybody" (1 Thessalonians 4:12). This means that no one will have a reason to accuse Christians of immature or worldly behavior. Living honorably has great value. Jesus' path is practical and simple and has no place for worldly living.

*Be careful to live properly among your
unbelieving neighbors. Then even if they accuse you
of doing wrong, they will see your honorable behavior,
and they will give honor to God when
He judges the world.*
1 Peter 2:12 NLT

*Who is wise and understanding among you?
Let them show it by their good life, by deeds done
in the humility that comes from wisdom.*
James 3:13

THE FULL MEASURE OF CHRIST'S LOVE

The word *growth* implies to grow up and reach maturity. This is the aim of all growth. Spiritual growth means to become spiritually mature. God knows the plans He has for you – that you would grow to the full measure of Christ's love so that you can love like He does. This is the highest fulfilment.

> *We continually ask God to fill you with the knowledge of His will through all the wisdom and understanding that the Spirit gives, so that you may live a life worthy of the Lord and please Him in every way: bearing fruit in every good work, growing in the knowledge of God.*
> Colossians 1:9-10

> *"Blessed are those who hunger and thirst for righteousness, for they will be filled."*
> Matthew 5:6

GROWTH BRINGS SATISFACTION

To be spiritually mature is to be like Christ. Jesus' maturity speaks of wisdom and responsibility. He lives out His relationship with the Father, and Jesus' satisfaction lies in doing what God asks. Like a father, God also desires to see us grow to maturity. There is great honor in attaining spiritual adulthood.

"My food," said Jesus, "is to do the will of Him
who sent Me and to finish His work."
John 4:34

Now He who supplies seed to the sower and bread for
food will also supply and increase your store of seed
and will enlarge the harvest of your righteousness.
2 Corinthians 9:10

NOT PRIDE, BUT LOVE

Spiritual growth is not just a matter of gaining knowledge and experience. This doesn't make one mature – rather, puffed up with pride, almost like a know-it-all teenager. There is so much restoration and healing in Christ as you develop, and so much love in Christ's maturity. Ask the Father to help you to grow to maturity in Christ.

Now about food sacrificed to idols: We know that
"We all possess knowledge." But knowledge puffs
up while love builds up.
1 Corinthians 8:1

Dear brothers and sisters, don't be
childish in your understanding of these things.
Be innocent as babies when it comes to evil,
but be mature in understanding
matters of this kind.
1 Corinthians 14:20 NLT

CHARACTER TRAITS

Jesus' character traits define spiritual maturity. These include love, joy, peace, patience, kindness, goodness, gentleness, faithfulness and self-control. It's good to take note that these are not gifts but character traits. You develop these qualities by patiently working on them, which takes resolution and determination. These traits flow from deep in the heart and are nurtured through perseverance.

The Holy Spirit produces this kind of fruit in our lives: love, joy, peace, patience, kindness, goodness, faithfulness, gentleness, and self-control. There is no law against these things!

Galatians 5:22-23 NLT

Giving all diligence, add to your faith virtue, to virtue knowledge, to knowledge self-control, to self-control perseverance, to perseverance godliness, to godliness, to godliness brotherly kindness, and to brotherly kindness love.

2 Peter 1:5-7 NKJV

THE POWER TO LIVE A GODLY LIFE

The wonderful news is that we have the ability to develop Jesus' character traits because we have been born again. God gave us enough divine power "for a godly life through our knowledge of Him who called us by His own glory and goodness" (2 Peter 1:3). We have the inborn ability to live a righteous life, but it only comes to the fore when we live in obedience to God and stay grafted to Jesus.

Instead, speaking the truth in love, we will grow to become in every respect the mature body of Him who is the head, that is, Christ. From Him the whole body, joined and held together by every supporting ligament, grows and builds itself up in love, as each part does its work.
Ephesians 4:15-16

For He chose us in Him before the creation of the world to be holy and blameless in His sight.
Ephesians 1:4

FULLY MATURE

I heard someone say that they were spiritually, but not emotionally, mature. This of course is impossible. To be spiritually mature implies that we are emotionally mature as well. To live in obedience to God doesn't involve mystical spiritual abilities that are removed from everyday life. It requires true maturity in all areas of our lives. We can only mature and become like Jesus if we allow Him access to our lives.

You also, like living stones, are being built into a spiritual house to be a holy priesthood, offering spiritual sacrifices acceptable to God through Jesus Christ.
1 Peter 2:5

… Built on the foundation of the apostles and prophets, with Christ Jesus Himself as the chief cornerstone. In Him the whole building is joined together and rises to become a holy temple in the Lord. And in Him you too are being built together to become a dwelling in which God lives by His Spirit.
Ephesians 2:20-22

SPIRITUAL GROWTH TAKES PERSEVERANCE

Spiritual growth doesn't happen by attending seminars and courses. Sitting in church for years also does not guarantee spiritual maturity. Spiritual growth only happens through complete obedience to the Word of God and the voice of Christ. Obedience is a choice. The Holy Spirit may tell you to forgive others, but only by persevering in obedience will Jesus' character traits become evident in your life.

Blessed is the one who does not walk in step with the wicked or stand in the way that sinners take or sit in the company of mockers, but whose delight is in the law of the LORD, and who meditates on His law day and night. That person is like a tree planted by streams of water, which yields its fruit in season and whose leaf does not wither – whatever they do prospers.

Psalm 1:1-3

LET GOD IN TODAY

By denying God access to your life you are opening the door for Satan. We must daily live in obedience so that Jesus' life becomes evident in us. Satan enters when we walk in the flesh. It doesn't help to live in the world and then pray fiery spiritual warfare prayers. We must allow Jesus to enter our lives. Only then will you experience victory and glory.

The flesh desires what is contrary to the Spirit,
and the Spirit what is contrary to the flesh. They are
in conflict with each other, so that you are not to
do whatever you want.
Galatians 5:17

When you follow the desires of your sinful nature,
the results are very clear: sexual immorality, impurity,
lustful pleasures … and other sins like these.
Let me tell you again, as I have before, that anyone living
that sort of life will not inherit the Kingdom of God.
Galatians 5:19, 21 NLT

CARRIERS OF LIGHT

Paul encouraged the believers by reminding them that God is in them. He works His desires into our hearts and equips us to do what He wants us to do. Listen to God – He is the hope of glory within us. To obey God's voice in our hearts makes us carriers of light. We don't give much weight to arguments and accolades because the light shines, regardless of these things. We must just be obedient and God will do the work.

For it is God who works in you to will and to
act in order to fulfill His good purpose.
Do everything without grumbling or arguing.
Philippians 2:13-14

He who began a good work in you will carry
it on to completion until the day of Christ Jesus.
Philippians 1:6

UNRESTRICTED ACCESS

When believers become quiet before God and worship Him, they will find that God works in them. He awakens His desires in us, sends us in the right direction and helps us to achieve our goals. He asks that we would allow Him to work in us without us trying to oppose Him. When we are born again we have the wonderful privilege of having the Almighty God put His trust in us and live through us. Give God unrestricted access to your life today.

Now may the God of peace, who through the blood of the eternal covenant brought back from the dead our Lord Jesus, that great Shepherd of the sheep, equip you with everything good for doing His will, and may He work in us what is pleasing to Him.
Hebrews 13:20-21

"On that day no one who is on the housetop, with possessions inside, should go down to get them. Likewise, no one in the field should go back for anything."
Luke 17:31

DECEMBER

HOMEWARD BOUND

*I saw "a new heaven and a new earth,"
for the first heaven and the first earth had
passed away, and there was no longer
any sea. Revelation 21:1*

THE KINGDOM OF GOD

God's kingdom is His dominion, His reign. He is the King and He sets the rules. There is no threat to God's kingdom and no other authority can overthrow it. When we pray, "Let Your kingdom …" it is the same as saying, "Let Your will be done." In heaven, God's will is perfectly carried out, but on earth we fall a bit short. Accept God's authority and live for Him.

"Your kingdom come, Your will be done, on earth as it is in heaven."

Matthew 6:10

The kingdom of God is not a matter of eating and drinking, but of righteousness, peace and joy in the Holy Spirit, because anyone who serves Christ in this way is pleasing to God and receives human approval.

Romans 14:17-18

A CHANGE OF NATURE

As humans we have a nature that constantly wants to rebel against God. We know that with this nature we are lost and we battle to dutifully carry out God's will. The solution to this problem is a change of character. And we can only achieve this change through Jesus who enters our hearts when we are born again. Pray that today you will accept God's authority and leadership over you. Thank Him for saving you and inviting you into His kingdom.

Jesus replied, "Very truly I tell you, no one can see the kingdom of God unless they are born again."
John 3:3

Jesus answered, "Most assuredly, I say to you, unless one is born again, he cannot see the kingdom of God."
John 3:5 NKJV

CHRIST BEARS OUR SINS

If we are rebellious to God, we deserve punishment. The penalty for our sins is death. If we are punished, there is no deliverance for us – this is because it is destined that each person dies once and is then judged. But God is merciful; He sent His own Son to bear the punishment for our sins. He was raised from the dead to give us life from God, and this life starts here on earth.

Just as people are destined to die once, and after that to face judgment, so Christ was sacrificed once to take away the sins of many; and He will appear a second time, not to bear sin, but to bring salvation to those who are waiting for Him.

Hebrews 9:27-28

He was pierced for our transgressions, He was crushed for our iniquities; the punishment that brought us peace was on Him, and by His wounds we are healed.

Isaiah 53:5

A NEW LIFE WITHIN

We don't automatically obtain a new life in Christ. We also don't receive it when we are baptized or by attending church. We receive it when we confess our sins to God and give our life to His Son so that we can be reconciled to Him. This happens when we accept Jesus Christ as our Lord and Savior – then the miracle takes place.

Yet to all who did receive Him, to those who believed in His name, He gave the right to become children of God – children born not of natural descent, nor of human decision or a husband's will, but born of God.
John 1:12-13

Once, on being asked by the Pharisees when the kingdom of God would come, Jesus replied, "The coming of the kingdom of God is not something that can be observed, nor will people say, 'Here it is,' or 'There it is,' because the kingdom of God is in your midst."
Luke 17:20-21

A NEW CREATION!

Jesus says that we are renewed by the Spirit of God, becoming a new person in Christ. The old nature is removed and we are given a new life through the Spirit. We are no longer condemned, but are free citizens in His kingdom.

"You should not be surprised at My saying, 'You must be born again.' The wind blows wherever it pleases. You hear its sound, but you cannot tell where it comes from or where it is going. So it is with everyone born of the Spirit."

John 3:7-8

Therefore, if anyone is in Christ, the new creation has come: The old has gone, the new is here!

2 Corinthians 5:17

HOMEWARD BOUND

Now that we are children of God, we are no longer sinners headed for hell. We are now homeward bound to our eternal home with the Father and the Son. We are part of God's kingdom and for the first time we are able to understand it. Isn't that a reason to celebrate?

Do you not know that wrongdoers will not inherit the kingdom of God? And that is what some of you were. But you were washed, you were sanctified, you were justified in the name of the Lord Jesus Christ and by the Spirit of our God.

1 Corinthians 6:9, 11

Set your mind on things above, not on earthly things. For you died, and your life is now hidden with Christ in God.

Colossians 3:2-3

CHILDREN OF THE KING!

A miracle happened when the Spirit of God made us new: We were no longer sinners bound for hell, but part of God's family. We are on the way to our eternal home, where we will share in His kingdom. What a privilege and a joy this is!

Dear friends, now we are children of God, and what we will be has not yet been made known. But we know that when Christ appears, we shall be like Him, for we shall see Him as He is.

1 John 3:2

See how very much our Father loves us, for He calls us His children, and that is what we are! But the people who belong to this world don't recognize that we are God's children because they don't know Him.

1 John 3:1 NLT

ALL ABOUT RELATIONSHIPS

Jesus defines everlasting life as a relationship rather than a period of time. The highest calling in life is to be united with Christ and to have a relationship with Him. The result of Jesus' ministry in people's lives is reconciliation – we are reconciled with Him and we are to reconcile with others. The outstanding characteristic of Jesus' disciples should be unconditional love for one another. This is the nature of relationship.

*All this is a gift from God, who brought us
back to Himself through Christ. And God
has given us the task of reconciling people to Him.*
2 Corinthians 5:8 NLT

*"A new command I give you: Love one another.
As I have loved you, so you must love one another.
By this everyone will know that you are My disciples,
if you love one another."*
John 13:34-35

CHOOSE JESUS AND LIVE!

If we are reconciled with Christ we are also reconciled with the Father. When we die, God lets us live for eternity with the choice we made while on earth. We are either going to spend eternity reconciled with Jesus and the Father or we are going to spend it banned from His presence. This decisive and pivotal decision is made this side of the grave. Now is the time to choose Jesus and to make the choice that has eternal consequences.

"Now this is eternal life: that they know You,
the only true God, and Jesus Christ,
whom You have sent."
John 17:3

This is the testimony: God has given us eternal life,
and this life is in His Son. Whoever has the
Son has life; whoever does not have the
Son of God does not have life.
1 John 5:11-12

MEMBERSHIP THAT COUNTS

If we choose to rebel against God's rule here on earth, we will have to live with that choice for all eternity. If we submit to Christ's authority, we will live for eternity with that decision. There are no churches in heaven and church membership means nothing. The only membership that counts is being a member of God's family. And that lasts for all time!

As for you, see that what you have heard from the beginning remains in you. If it does, you also will remain in the Son and in the Father. This is what He promised us – eternal life.
1 John 2:24-25

For the wages of sin is death, but the gift of God is eternal life in Christ Jesus our Lord.
Romans 6:23

THANKS BE TO GOD!

Take a few moments to thank Jesus for the eternal life you have received through Him. Thank Him that you have been reconciled with God and that you can spend eternity in your Father's house. Surely there is no greater joy than this!

Praise be to the God and Father of our Lord Jesus Christ! In His great mercy He has given us new birth into a living hope through the resurrection of Jesus Christ from the dead, and into an inheritance that can never perish, spoil or fade. This inheritance is kept in heaven for you.
1 Peter 1:3-4

The sting of death is sin, and the power of sin is the law. But thanks be to God! He gives us the victory through our Lord Jesus Christ.
1 Corinthians 15:56-57

JESUS IS THE WAY

Eternal life is not about a very long period of time, but about relationship. Anyone who stands in a relationship with God through Jesus has eternal life. There is no way to get to heaven except through Jesus. God loved us so much that He sacrificed His very own Son to open the way between Him and us.

Jesus answered, "I am the way and the truth and the life. No one comes to the Father except through Me."

John 14:6

"This is how God loved the world: He gave His one and only Son, so that everyone who believes in Him will not perish but have eternal life. God sent His Son into the world not to judge the world, but to save the world through Him."

John 3:16-17 NLT

ARE YOU SURE?

If you are unsure whether you are heading for an eternity with God, ask yourself the following questions: Is Jesus my Lord and Savior? Am I in a relationship with God through Jesus Christ? Have I got the new life of Christ in me?

If you are sure of your answers, you can be sure of your eternal destination. If you are not sure, make sure, because now is the time; tomorrow might be too late.

Everyone who calls on the name of
the Lord will be saved.
Romans 10:13

If you declare with your mouth, "Jesus is Lord," and
believe in your heart that God raised Him from the
dead, you will be saved. For it is with your heart that
you believe and are justified, and it is with your mouth
that you profess your faith and are saved.
Romans 10:9-10

LIVING FOR ETERNITY

The thought of spending an eternity with our Father is so wonderful and awe-inspiring. Meditate on these verses today and thank Jesus for your new life in Him and for the reconciliation that has taken place in your life.

"Here is the bread that comes down from heaven, which anyone may eat and not die. I am the living bread that came down from heaven. Whoever eats this bread will live forever. This bread is My flesh, which I will give for the life of the world."
John 6:50-51

"Not everyone who calls out to Me, 'Lord! Lord!' will enter the Kingdom of Heaven. Only those who actually do the will of My Father in heaven will enter."
Matthew 7:21 NLT

DEAD YET ALIVE

Death is a forbidding force in the life of every person and in the presence of death even Jesus becomes small in some people's eyes. It's as if we have full confidence that Jesus can do something while the person is alive, but when they die even Jesus can't do anything. This is not true, because all who believe in Jesus will live even though they die.

Jesus told her, "I am the resurrection and the life. Anyone who believes in Me will live, even after dying. Everyone who lives in Me and believes in Me will never ever die. Do you believe this, Martha?"
John 11:25-26 NLT

Do not be deceived: God cannot be mocked. A man reaps what he sows. Whoever sows to please their flesh, from the flesh will reap destruction; whoever sows to please the Spirit, from the Spirit will reap eternal life.
Galatians 6:7-8

DEATH HAS BEEN CONQUERED

Focus on these comforting verses today and thank God for overcoming death and for preparing a place in heaven for us, where death will have no power over us.

When the perishable has been clothed with
the imperishable, and the mortal with immortality,
then the saying that is written will come true:
"Death has been swallowed up in victory."
"Where, O death, is your victory?
Where, O death, is your sting?"
1 Corinthians 15:54-55

"Do not let your hearts be troubled.
You believe in God; believe also in Me.
My Father's house has many rooms; if that
were not so, would I have told you that I am
going there to prepare a place for you?
And if I go and prepare a place for you,
I will come back and take you to be with
Me that you also may be where I am."
John 14:1-3

DEATH NO LONGER A THREAT

When we realize that Jesus has the final victory over death, we begin to see death in a new light. We know that it won't have a hold on us and that it is simply the bridge between us and our Father. We also know that we will see other believers and loved ones again when we are all united in heaven.

"Do not be afraid. I am the First and the Last. I am the Living One; I was dead, and now look, I am alive for ever and ever! And I hold the keys of death and Hades."
Revelation 1:17-18

I heard a loud voice from the throne saying, "Look! God's dwelling place is now among the people, and He will dwell with them. They will be His people, and God Himself will be with them and be their God. 'He will wipe every tear from their eyes. There will be no more death' or mourning or crying or pain, for the old order of things has passed away."
Revelation 21:3-4

WE HAVE HOPE

There is hope even in the cruel presence of death. As believers we don't need to desperately cling to life as if there is no life after death. Everyone who is in Christ Jesus has life within them. Even in the face of death, believers have all the courage in the world. We don't grieve like the unsaved because Jesus is all we need.

Brothers and sisters, we do not want you to
be uninformed about those who sleep
in death, so that you do not grieve like
the rest of mankind, who have no hope.
1 Thessalonians 4:13

Therefore we do not lose heart. Though outwardly
we are wasting away, yet inwardly we are being
renewed day by day. For our light and momentary
troubles are achieving for us an eternal glory
that far outweighs them all.
2 Corinthians 4:16-17

GOD HAS DEFEATED THE DEVIL

Some people picture God and the devil fighting over a person's soul. This isn't accurate, because God has already won the battle through Jesus and His death on the cross. Jesus stripped the devil of his rank as commanding officer when He defeated him on the cross. Through His death, Jesus also destroyed the dossier of allegations against us. There is no ongoing battle between God and the devil because God has already won.

Having disarmed the powers and authorities,
He made a public spectacle of them,
triumphing over them by the cross.
Colossians 2:15

Our struggle is not against flesh and blood, but
against the rulers, against the authorities, against the
powers of this dark world and against the
spiritual forces of evil in the
heavenly realms.
Ephesians 6:12

FIX YOUR EYES ON JESUS

There is a battle raging, but it is not between God and the devil. It is between God's followers and the evil one. The devil tries vehemently to destroy and smother the testimony of the living Body of Christ. In the New Testament, Jesus' disciples are told to resist the devil and to overcome him through remaining faithful to Jesus. Remain in Jesus and persevere to the end.

Therefore, since we are surrounded by such a great cloud of witnesses, let us throw off everything that hinders and the sin that so easily entangles. And let us run with perseverance the race marked out for us, fixing our eyes on Jesus, the pioneer and perfecter of faith. For the joy set before Him He endured the cross, scorning its shame, and sat down at the right hand of the throne of God.
Hebrews 12:1-2

Do you not know that in a race all the runners run, but only one gets the prize? Run in such a way as to get the prize.
1 Corinthians 9:24

GOD HAS WON!

The devil can never win. He can destroy, but he can never win. The power and glory Satan speaks about in Matthew 4 have been taken from him and the victory is clearly God's. God is the victor and we live in that victory by remaining in Christ.

Again, the devil took Him to a very high mountain and showed Him all the kingdoms of the world and their splendor. "All this I will give you," he said, "if you will bow down and worship me." Jesus said to him, "Away from Me, Satan! For it is written: 'Worship the Lord your God, and serve Him only.'"

Matthew 4:8-10

Thanks be to God! He gives us the victory through our Lord Jesus Christ.

1 Corinthians 15:57

SATAN HAS LOST THE BATTLE

The Bible tells us that the believers conquer Satan through the blood of the lamb and the word of their testimony, even when they are martyred. Jesus broke the power of death for every child of God. Jesus' death was the victory over evil.

Believers can never be defeated, even if they are put to death. Death is not the end because the same Spirit who raised Jesus from the dead is present in every believer and will raise their bodies to eternal life.

"For the accuser of our brothers and sisters,
who accuses them before our God day and night,
has been hurled down. They triumphed over him by the
blood of the Lamb and by the word of their testimony;
they did not love their lives so much as to shrink from
death. Therefore rejoice, you heavens and you who dwell
in them! But woe to the earth and the sea, because the
devil has gone down to you! He is filled with fury,
because he knows that his time is short."
Revelation 12:10-12

REMAIN FAITHFUL TO JESUS

The devil can try to smother the church's testimony for a while, but what he does will always be exposed by God. It doesn't matter if believers live or die, they defeat the devil by remaining faithful to Jesus. Jesus is present and real in the life of every believer, every day, in every way, in every place all over the earth.

God saved you by His grace when you believed.
And you can't take credit for this; it is a gift from God.
Salvation is not a reward for the good things we have
done, so none of us can boast about it.
Ephesians 2:8-9 NLT

God "will repay each person according
to what they have done."
Romans 2:6

DON'T BE TOO PROUD

Sometimes we start off thinking that we can solve our problems with courage and zeal, but then we realize that we are in trouble. Some are wise enough to acknowledge this and look for help, but others are too proud and carry on as if they have everything under control. This is foolish because we find victory and healing in Christ.

We don't need to be burdened with disobedience, wounds, lies and other problems. We can be free – if we would just stop being too proud to ask for help. As believers, we have the Holy Spirit to help us and guide us until we get to heaven.

Pride leads to disgrace, but with humility comes wisdom.
Proverbs 11:2 NLT

"The Helper, the Holy Spirit, whom the Father
will send in My name, He will teach you all things,
and bring to your remembrance
all things that I said to you."
John 14:26 NKJV

A REWARD IN HEAVEN

While we are still on this earth we need run the race with our eyes fixed on Jesus. When we finish the race there is a reward that awaits us in heaven. Ask Jesus to help you throw off the things that hinder you from finishing the race and confess your sins to Him. What lies beyond the finish line is worth the perseverance and pain of the race.

Therefore we do not lose heart.
Though outwardly we are wasting away,
yet inwardly we are being renewed day by day.
2 Corinthians 4:16

"Do not be afraid of what you are about to suffer.
I tell you, the devil will put some of you in prison to
test you, and you will suffer persecution for ten days.
Be faithful, even to the point of death, and I will
give you life as your victor's crown."
Revelation 2:10

PERSEVERE UNTIL THE END

We will always be surrounded by sin until we die or until Jesus comes again. We need to persevere and keep our eyes on Jesus until that day. This is the path of discipleship and it is an ongoing journey. Never despair, because the second coming of Jesus and our perfect redemption are at hand.

The night is nearly over; the day is almost here. So let us put aside the deeds of darkness and put on the armor of light. Let us behave decently, as in the daytime, not in carousing and drunkenness, not in sexual immorality and debauchery, not in dissension and jealousy.
Romans 13:12-13

Therefore, get rid of all moral filth and the evil that is so prevalent and humbly accept the word planted in you, which can save you.
James 1:21

CHRIST IS THE VICTOR

Of all the things we are most afraid of, death surely tops the list. Even though we might escape everything else, we cannot escape death. We accept it as final and non-negotiable. As Christians we need to remember that Jesus is Lord and He has conquered death. Jesus is real; He isn't a philosophy or a fable. He is the Victor over death.

The last enemy to be destroyed is death.
1 Corinthians 15:26

"Do not be amazed at this, for a time is coming when all who are in their graves will hear His voice and come out – those who have done what is good will rise to live, and those who have done what is evil will rise to be condemned."
John 5:28-29

DON'T DELAY!

Having a Christian burial won't save you and ensure you go to heaven. You can't be saved after you die. Your eternal destination is decided before you die, whether you are ready for it or not. Don't put off the decision to ask God to save you. If you die without God, you will face His judgment and an eternity without Him.

God "will repay each person according to what they have done." To those who by persistence in doing good seek glory, honor and immortality, He will give eternal life. But for those who are self-seeking and who reject the truth and follow evil, there will be wrath and anger."

Romans 2:6-8

"But understand this: If the owner of the house had known at what hour the thief was coming, he would not have let his house be broken into."

Luke 12:39

A CHOICE WITH ETERNAL CONSEQUENCES

Jesus told the parable of the rich man in hell who begged Lazarus and Abraham for a drop of water (see Luke 16:19-31). It is clear that the rich man had no way of escaping and that there was no chance of salvation. The rich man had had his chance to choose Jesus and live, but he chose death. Are you ready to face God? Have you decided whom you will follow?

"In Hades, where he was in torment, he looked up and saw Abraham far away, with Lazarus by his side. So he called to him, 'Father Abraham, have pity on me and send Lazarus to dip the tip of his finger in water and cool my tongue, because I am in agony in this fire.'"

Luke 16:23-24

"Look, I come like a thief! Blessed is the one who stays awake and remains clothed, so as not to go naked and be shamefully exposed."

Revelation 16:15

THE FATHER'S BOSOM

In John's gospel we read that Jesus came from the Father's bosom. The moment we reach out to Jesus and embrace Him with our life, He takes us with Him to the place He comes from – the Father's bosom. This doesn't happen at the Second Coming; it already took place when we were born again. It is then that we became temples of the living God.

No one has ever seen God, but the one and only Son, who is Himself God and is in closest relationship with the Father, has made Him known.
John 1:18

Do you not know that you are the temple of God and that the Spirit of God dwells in you?
1 Corinthians 3:16 NKJV

HEIRS FOR ETERNITY

We are already hidden with Christ in God (see Colossians 3:3). This is a wonderful truth because it speaks of the inheritance from God in which we can partake. The greatest inheritance we can receive is a place in the Father's bosom. That which was allotted to Christ is now available to all who believe in the Son. We are heirs with the Father and joint heirs with the Son.

He saved us, not because of righteous things we had done, but because of His mercy. He saved us through the washing of rebirth and renewal by the Holy Spirit, whom He poured out on us generously through Jesus Christ our Savior, so that, having been justified by His grace, we might become heirs having the hope of eternal life.

Titus 3:5-7

Praise be to the God and Father of our Lord Jesus Christ! In His great mercy He has given us new birth into a living hope through the resurrection of Jesus Christ from the dead.

1 Peter 1:3